THE ISLAND OF ARRAN

Copyright © 2001 Ben Capulford

First Published : Dec 2001

ISBN: 0-9541569-0-0

Written By : Ben Capulford

Published By: Arran Graphics & Computers Ltd

Distribution By: Arran Graphics & Computers Ltd

Printed in the UK by RCS plc.

Artwork:
Original Cover Artwork: J.C. Mills
Cartoons: R. Duncan / Ben Capulford
Digital Artwork (cover): Ben Capulford

Sustenance: Isle of Arran Brewery

All rights reserved. No part of this publication may be reproduced, stored in a retrieval system, or transmitted, in any form or by any means, electronic or mechanical, by photocopying, recording or otherwise, without prior permission in writing by the publisher.

The author and publishers have done their best to ensure the accuracy and currency of all the information in this book. However, they cannot accept any responsibility for any loss, injury or inconvenience sustained by anyone as a result of information contained within this guidebook.

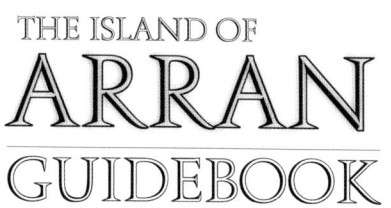

To Zoë

"Tide's Out"

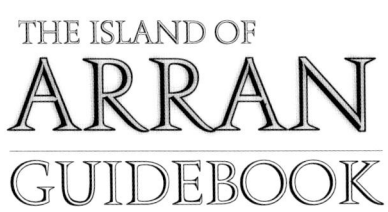

FOREWORD

The Island of Arran is briefly mentioned in many new-age guidebooks and this format for the modern-day traveller is a style that I wished to emulate as a basis for this publication. These globally-available guidebooks are usually involved in covering Scotland (or even the entire UK) as a whole and Arran often finds itself allocated to a page or two as an island with a castle, two ferry links and several red deer. Those who live on Arran, of course, know it to be much more than that and even regular visitors to the island find new places to go, new businesses opening up and therefore always a different holiday.

This book, therefore, contains much in the way of factual information but it is also a personal guide and should be taken in that light. I hope that after reading this book you will find, as I do, that Arran comes across as an island that stands out from the rest of Scotland in a very positive way.

There are important points to bear in mind as you read this book. The familiar phrase "all information was correct at the time of going to press" is certainly valid. Visitors should note that Arran business hours are often seasonal, holidays are staggered throughout the year and the timing of many events do not fall on specific dates, but are adjusted in order not to clash with other local "goings on". Also of note is the occasional demise of businesses, a change in their 'modus operandi' or change of ownership that, for obvious reasons, was not known of at the time this book was printed.

Another well-worn cliché "See Local Press" will appear often in the guide. Where I can illustrate what goes on, precise dates and times should always be confirmed either with the local newspaper, the Arran Banner, or with event organisers themselves.

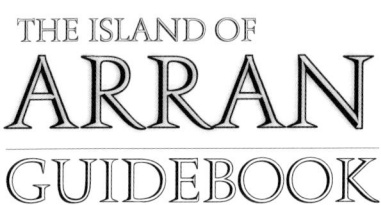

I regret these seemingly obvious excuses to give up on parts of my research, but this has been unavoidable in most cases. Such is the nature of this type of publication. As an attempt to combat this, contact details have been given wherever possible.

Also, with the development of low-cost computer technology and the huge increase of Internet and email use, it was an easy decision to transfer the majority of information in this book to a format which could be accessed on computer. The PC-formatted CD Rom which has been designed in conjunction with the book includes website links to many Arran businesses, over 200 photographs, two enjoyable films of Arran and audio tracks - something which would have been impossible to put on a conventional website.

Any future editions of the book will hopefully include feedback from travellers and visitors to the island and if you would like to comment on any matter, please feel free to contact me through email. Naturally, I am oriented towards positive tourism development, constructive criticism and your own personal experiences.

I hope you enjoy Arran,

Ben Capulford,
Isle of Arran.

email: **bencapulford@hotmail.com**

USING THE GUIDEBOOK

The Island of Arran Guidebook is laid out into three distinct sections.

SECTION 1
A detailed description of the island, it's general services and other useful information is found within the first section

SECTION 2
There are very detailed analyses on each village area and the attractions and facilities within that particular village. For a fuller list of accommodation providers in each village area, contact the tourist board on 01770 302140 (www.ayrshire-arran.co.uk). Other websites that link to agencies and tourism businesses are shown on the CD Rom.

SECTION 3
A number of pages dedicated to checklists of popular attractions, visitor centres, walks and other Arran specialities. These are intended to provide a quick reference to visitors who "don't want to miss anything". They will also help, I hope, to plan your day - whether it's going to be an outdoor one, or otherwise. Also here are pages of FAQs (frequently asked questions), village maps, and a page dedicated to Arran Trivia.

THE ISLAND OF ARRAN GUIDEBOOK

CONTENTS

Arran - Introduction	**11**
How to get to Arran	**14**
Arran's Roads & Getting Around	**16**
Eating In...or Out	**20**
Where to Stay	**21**
Arran's Climate	**25**
Finding Out 'What's On'	**26**
Arran's Wildlife	**29**
Local Services	**32**
Village Sections:	
Brodick	39
Lamlash	52
Whiting Bay	56
Corrie & Sannox	60
Lochranza & Catacol	65
Shiskine & Blackwaterfoot	70
The West Coast	75
Kildonan & Kilmory	79
Sliddery & Corriecravie	82
Village Maps/Arran Map	**83/89**
FAQs	**90**
Mountain Ridges (peaks)	**92**
Arran Trivia	**93**
Visitor Centre Checklist	**94**
Further Reading	**95**
Index	**97**
Spotters Notes	**99**

THE ISLAND OF ARRAN

Arran lies about 14 miles of the western coastline of southern Scotland, 30 miles southwest of Glasgow and protected from the assault of the Atlantic Ocean by the long peninsula of Kintyre, Argyll. Approximately 60 miles in circumference and just under 200 square miles in size, Arran is one of the larger Scottish isles, not quite within the "hebridean chains" geographically, but unique as the most accessible of Scotland's holiday islands.

The resident population of around 4,500 is made up of native Scottish and English, with noticeable numbers of summer residents from many parts of the world. The tourism and business industries account for an influx of around 300,000 visitors every year.

Arran's main road, the A841, runs almost all way around the coast, connecting the villages. All but one of these villages are situated on the coast; Shiskine being the exception, which lies on the "String Road", the B880, a cross-island route. The other inland road is known locally as the "Ross Road" and connects Lamlash with Kilmory.

The island is made up of three large villages (with populations of up to 1,000 or more) and many smaller communities of around 50 to 250 residents. The larger villages of Brodick, Lamlash and Whiting Bay are well-serviced with Brodick being the most functional because of its two banks, the major post office and larger supermarkets. Almost all villages, however, have their own stores and post office and Arran benefits from many local service vans providing anything from meat deliveries to banking facilities.

Don't go to Arran looking for Aran Sweaters. *That* Aran lies off the coast of Ireland. Also, be aware that to "do Arran in a day" is not really possible. Of course, you can easily drive around the entire coast road in about 3 hours, but allowing for the chances to get out and explore, take a walk in the hills and visit the established attractions of the island surely demands more time.

ARRAN AS A TOURIST DESTINATION.

For the once-a-year visitor the island is an easily accessible destination, seemingly far from the large towns and cities of the mainland (though it's actually very close). It's also a place of very mixed scenery, compacted into two hundred square miles and designed as if it was initially created to be an "area of natural beauty". The ruggedness of the natural features forces the island into a terminal state of 'olde-worldeness' - the modernising of roads being almost impossible in some areas and the restoration of many original cottages and houses adds to this authenticity, whilst planning permission for large scale business developments of any kind is often withheld, argued and criticised in view of the island's identity as a showcase for Scotland's natural assets.

Whether this is good or bad for the island's economy depends on your point-of-view. However, the tourism industry thrives on Arran for one reason - few people who live on the island could maintain their current lifestyle without it. In recent years, tourism has supplied the need for extensive new facilities, a wider range of services and many small enterprises have been set up just about everywhere as the island subtly manoeuvres itself into the perceived trends of the 21st century.

The six-month 'high season' from May to October is a world apart from the long winter, but as most people who visit Arran are predominantly interested in being outside, the chance to walk, hike, cycle and explore are very much year-round attractions. Nevertheless, there is much more to do in the summer, the weather is usually fair and the wildlife is extremely varied. Winter brings the occasional storm, some businesses go into hibernation and it is more the time of year to come if you are a particularly 'avid' outdoor enthusiast or you simply want to wrap up in front of a log fire and write your memoirs.

Arran's flora and fauna are diverse and, in some cases, rare. The island benefits from resident golden eagles, red deer and otters - whilst summer visitors include basking sharks, dolphins and, on very infrequent occasions, whales. For the horticulturally minded, rhododendrons are just about everywhere, but rare ferns, palm trees and orchids are also to be found at various sites throughout the island.

The warm gulf-stream winds and currents bring a climate which is suitable for these unusual plants and animals, so that Arran is often astoundingly different from your expectations of what a western Scottish island is like.

Tourism trends are changing, however, as travellers from America, Europe and further afield use the island as a convenient starting point or final destination on a more general tour of Scotland. Whilst islanders and their businesses try to entice people to stay longer, there has been a noticeable development in the number of businesses recognising the "two-day-tripper". These are generally tourists who stay on the island for around 36 hours, often making use of the ferry services which operate in two separate areas of the island. These visitors include a large increase in European coach tours that tend to visit the castle and other larger businesses on their hebridean tour.

British tourists also flock to Arran and many come year after year, staying in the same self-catering unit or bed and breakfast house. This is crucial to the economy and helps to maintain a second income for some households. However, with the huge increase in inexpensive European holidays and well-established long-haul flights that are now within the budget of a much larger proportion of the British population, the domestic holiday market is a battlefield of marketing campaigns, fought between the various tourist authorities.

There is also an increasing number of people coming to Arran in order to buy their own holiday home which they use like a time-share, taking a holiday on the island themselves for several weeks, whilst renting it out their property when they are not on the island. This is now big business in the self-catering world on Arran and at least two agencies have a large number of properties on their books, for clients who live elsewhere in Britain or overseas.

Facilities on the island for all ages are generally well-developed and there are many activities to keep children and adults entertained for a lengthened stay on the island. These are detailed throughout the book.

HOW TO GET TO ARRAN

Ferry Services

Unless you are lucky enough to have your own cruiser or yacht, you can only reach Arran by ferry. The ferry company - there is only one at present - is Caledonian MacBrayne Scottish Ferries who control all passenger transport of a sea-going nature throughout the western isles of Scotland (P & O only run the northern isles to Orkney and Shetland). This makes things easy in one sense (especially for bookings) but it also means that you will have to pay around £60 for a family car with two people (return). For most, it's a justifiable travel expense, especially if you are staying for the average 7 - night holiday and there are money-saving six-journey tickets for those who use the service more frequently throughout the year. The ferry service between Claonaig and Lochranza is slightly cheaper, but it's a long road around Loch Lomond for the £10 or so that you'll save and really not worth it unless you are arriving from the north of Scotland or the western isles.

Ardrossan, the harbour town that you'll need to drive through to reach the main terminal is easy enough to find. Just off the A78 from Irvine (a surprisingly modern road and a very fast thoroughfare from Ayr up the western coast to Gourock) Ardrossan is a fairly dull place and yet has one main advantage for car drivers and that is that petrol is around 10 - 15p per litre *cheaper* here than on Arran, so fill up if you have the time.

The ferry terminal is located, obviously, on the seafront, and you would feel by the approach road that you were entering an industrial area, though this soon gives way to signs for "Arran Ferry". The first left after you cross the rail tracks is the long-stay car park which you will need to enter only if you intend arriving on foot. The ferry queue is the second left, manned by a small booth where someone will ask if you have booked or not and will also need your tickets. If you haven't booked, don't panic. The chances of getting aboard are around 50/50 at worst. If you don't have tickets, you should drive to the terminal at the end of the road before entering the ferry queue. You can purchase tickets here, as well as make general enquiries, telephone calls and so on. In any event, always try to turn up at least 30 minutes before the scheduled sailing time. If you haven't booked, arriving early will increase your chances of getting aboard sooner.

On the Claonaig ferry, most of the above services don't exist. You can't book - there's no terminal - just a slipway and the only services you'll find are telephone and toilets. You buy your ferry ticket on-board and the ferry itself has no on-board facilities except for washrooms.

The Ardrossan- Brodick crossing

The "Caledonian Isles" takes over 100 cars but there are many larger vehicles such as coaches and trucks that use the ferry on each crossing. A "mezzanine" deck operates in the summer, increasing the capacity. On the main deck are several lounges and seating areas, washrooms, a bar, a colourful cafeteria serving meals throughout the day and a restaurant that is less used. You can stroll around outside or sit on the top deck if the weather suits. There is a non-smoking policy throughout the ferry, except for the outside decks.
Crossing Time: 55 minutes. Regularity: 4 or 5 sailings per day (depends on day and time of year). Tel: 08705 650000 for more information and bookings. You can also book online through www.calmac.co.uk, but you still have to collect your tickets at the terminal from which you are departing.

The Claonaig- Lochranza crossing

Usually the "Loch Tarbert" taking just 17 or 18 cars. Occasionally tour coaches try to use the ferry but often get stuck mid-way on the slipway and there is mild panic and confusion as pieces of wood are jammed under the wheels as the vehicle is raised to get aboard! You can either sit in your car (only recommended if you don't want to see the wonderful views) or in a small seating area alongside the car deck. Best of all is to sit on the top deck and look for seals, sharks and porpoises which regularly swim up and down this stretch of water.
Crossing Time: 35 mins Regularity: 10 or 12 sailings per day. Tel 08705 650000 for info. Bookings not available. Summer only. Occasionally diverted to "Tarbert" in rough weather.

Getting to the ferry terminals

Trains run to Ardrossan harbour from Glasgow Central and are timed to coincide with the ferry sailings. The train journey takes just under an hour. Both Prestwick and Glasgow Airports are within easy reach, with excellent train connections to the harbour.

By road from Glasgow, you have a choice of several routes which each take just under an hour, whereas from England, your normal approach would be to use the M74 to just south of Glasgow and connect with the A71 to Irvine, via Kilmarnock, then the A78 to Ardrossan. Ardrossan Harbour is about an hour by road from the A71/M74 junction which is a further hour and a half from the English border.

ARRAN'S ROADS

The A841, Arran's "main road" skirts most of the coastline - a round trip of 57 miles. Apart from it's classification as an "A" class road, there is no similarity here than almost any other similarly designated road in Britain. Generally the road is very narrow in comparison to what you might expect, but most noticeably are the potholes, sharp bends, and natural "speed bumps" at the most unexpected places. Driving around the island can be exhilarating in every sense of the word. However, drivers who keep their eyes on the road will give their passengers a great trip around this island of diversity. There are plenty of places of stop well off the road (and so out of danger from other drivers) so if you do spot something that needs further attention (sharks, seals and deer are favourites) make sure you've not stopped just short of a blind corner. It's nearly impossible to achieve the national speed limit of 60mph (safely) anywhere around the island and, generally, you can expect to average around 30mph if you were to travel around the entire coastline. A handy guide, therefore, would be to take any mileage figure represented on maps or signs and double it for an estimation of the time it will take to get to the destination (eg: Brodick to Lochranza is 14 miles, allow around 28 minutes; Lamlash to Brodick is just 3 miles, allow 6 minutes and so on).

There are several stretches of road that need particular mention because of their 'uniqueness'.

The String & Ross Roads.

Arran also has two roads that cross the island. The String Road between Brodick and Blackwaterfoot is a popular route and saves a great deal of time if you are travelling from east to west or vice versa. It traverses a high range of hills, just south of the more dominant mountains of Goatfell and Cir Mhor. Nevertheless, it's a scenic route (especially going from west to east as the view of Brodick from the top is outstanding) and there are a few places to stop and look for eagles. Recent roadworks (where water pipes have been laid) have helped to improve parts of the road but there are still scars on the landscape, which will soon heal over with grass and heather. The String road also goes straight through the Shiskine Valley and the village of Shiskine itself is a well strung-out community and the only village on Arran that is not located on the coast. Blink, and you'll miss the only part of Arran's graded roads which has an 'oncoming traffic priority' section less than 20 yards long!

Access to the String road can be found just north of Brodick at a main junction where the A841 heads north to Corrie, Sannox and Lochranza. At the western end, the road re-joins the A841 just outside Blackwaterfoot at a well-signposted junction.

Two small spur roads cross over Machrie Moor from the String Road and these are helpful if you are planning to drive from, for example, Brodick to Dougarie.

The Ross Road is the quietest section of road on the island. Joining Lamlash to Kilmory and Sliddery in the south, it's a thin stretch of road with passing places. Although you shouldn't park in these areas, there are other places where you can stop and get out of the car to enjoy the quietest area of the island. Views to Holy Isle are very good from this short section of road and, like the String road, you have a good chance of seeing birds of prey (although they are more likely to be owls and buzzards rather than eagles). There is no bus service on the Ross road.

GETTING AROUND

The size of the island is perfect for just about any kind of travel mode that you care to use. Clearly, the most practical method is by car if you simply want to get from 'a to b', but there are increasing numbers of cyclists and walkers who also use the roads, especially in the busier peak season. Many visitors rely on the bus services too, which are fairly frequent in mid season and are generally timed to coincide with ferry arrivals and departures.

Public Transport

To catch a bus on Arran, you don't need to be standing at a bus stop unless you are in one of the major villages or you want to get out of the rain.. Most rural areas in fact do not have bus stops and the procedure to get aboard is simply to stand on the side of the road and wave your hand in the air, as if hailing a cab. It's a good idea to wait until a bus is visible first! Fares are determined on how far you are going and loose change is welcomed. School buses are exactly the same ones as used for public transport. On odd occasions, a bus will not pick you up simply because it is privately chartered by a school or other party but this does not affect the regular timetables which are freely available at the ferry terminal and the tourist office. An open-top tour bus offers the chance to see Arran from the top deck. This service, although enjoyable, only travels between Brodick and Whiting Bay so don't assume you're getting a full round-island ticket.

There are a few local taxi companies operating in Lamlash and Brodick. A & C Hendry (Brodick 302274) run cars and minibuses for any occasion. They also conduct tours of the island, which are well advertised on the ferry and at the pier. Arran Private Hire operates taxi services for the island from it's Lamlash HQ (tel: 600903).

Post Buses

The post office offers the chance of a lift around the island in one of their post vans should you be stuck for other means. Timetables are available from the Parcel Office in Brodick.

Cycling

Families often bring their bicycles to Arran and from May to September there are often more cyclists on the road than anything else. The increase, too, of cycle hire facilities in many of the villages adds to this growing trend. Keen cyclists can quite easily ride around the island in a day but there are several parts where high hills and hazardous stretches can be too intimidating for the general holiday-maker. In particular are the String Road and The Boguillie, where it is common to see a whole army of people walking their bicycles up the steep hills, whilst sweating profusely. However, the freewheeling trip down is well worth it once you reach the top! Always remember that at the bottom of the hill on which you are free-wheeling at 40mph down, there is usually a very sharp bend!

Cars & Car Hire

Having a car is by far the most preferable method of getting around the island for most people. The hazards, as mentioned, can be a little frustrating but it's the only way to have full access to all the island, when you want it. Many stopping places are overcrowded (Machrie Standing Stones car park and Merkland Shore, Brodick are often full) so it's often wise to have an alternative itinerary rather than trying to park on the road.

Petrol stations are easy enough to find in the south and Brodick has two petrol stations (one behind Alldays supermarket and the other at the pier). The pumps at Alldays also include LPG gas. There are no facilities anywhere north of the String road, so if you are planning to stay two weeks in Lochranza, for example, you will have to fill when you can, in Brodick or Blackwaterfoot (a thirty mile round trip from Lochranza). It's a good idea to have a spare gallon in a plastic can. If you're really stuck, your hotelier or the local shop may know someone locally with a spare litre or so!

If you decide to visit an area by car which is off the main roads, you should ask locally where the best place to park is as many areas are used by farm traffic in the south end in particular.

Recently, Arran Transport has set up a car hire facility at the pier in Brodick (tel: 302121).

Hitch-hiking

Relatively safe and frequently successful, hitch-hiking is a common pasttime amongst visitors and, indeed, locals. However, if you're thinking about it, bear in mind your location on the road and the possible dangers for stopping a vehicle on a blind corner.

EATING OUT...OR IN.

Throughout the island there are many places to eat and drink. Arran has no brand-named establishments and almost all restaurants and cafeterias are privately owned. This lack of instant recognition from the public's eyes has generally improved the overall range of food on offer, restrained only by availability of produce and the talents of the owners and chefs.

Local produce is very popular with both those who cook it and those who eat it. However, it is the most surprising items that carry the "locally made" mark, rather than the expected delicacies.

The joys of "eating in"

Fresh fish is, of course, available and even if it has not been caught locally, it won't have travelled far. Popular is fresh salmon (from neighbouring Loch Fyne), smoked salmon and, of course, venison which is often from a local animal.

Other relatively new additions to Arran's produce include Arran Dairy Ice Cream, a Chocolate Factory, the new Brewery and so on. These are mentioned in greater detail in the relevant village section.

WHERE TO STAY ON ARRAN

Where to stay depends largely on the duration of your visit. If you intend to stay a week or two, you can opt for the popular self-catering approach. There are a great deal of self-catering units on the island, most of which get booked early in the season. These are normally booked from Saturday to Saturday. Bed and Breakfast establishments which are privately run will often favour guests who are booking for more than one night, due to running costs. There are, however, exceptions.

There are also a great many hotels and guest houses on the island, two youth hostels and some well-serviced caravan and camping sites.

The rating system for Scottish accommodation and the tourist boards.

At the time of going to press there is no obligation for a residential establishment to hold a certain grading from the Scottish Tourist Board (the "STB"). This simply means that not all premises on Arran will be a member of the board. Why an increasing number of premises choose to decline membership is the subject of great discussion throughout the country. The Scottish Tourist Board has had a fairly rough ride in recent years, partly because of it's management structure and mostly because of it's rather confusing grading system. In the past few years, the board has tried using it's "crown system", the "star rating" (the current scheme) and even looked at "diamond-rating". Within the present star-rating scheme, each of the 5 categories (1 5 stars) is then sub-divided into types of accommodation such as hotel, small hotel, bed and breakfast and so on. Although seldom necessary, a further classification within each rating has been used, when required by the board, to determine whether a premises is, for example, a 5-star deluxe or 'merely' a 5-star operation. These star-ratings, by the way, are not to be considered parallel to other ratings schemes. An STB 3-star property, for example, will not necessarily be an AA 3-star.

Membership for establishments is often considered to be prohibitively expensive (therefore many bed and breakfast caterers simply decline), new owners have been known to wait up to 12 months to be graded and the grading scheme itself often asks for certain services and facilities that the owner of the premises feels are unnecessary, for reasons of viability or necessity.

Visitors should, therefore, not assume that a premises which is not a member of the Scottish Tourist Board is not a good place to stay. By far the best way to ascertain the quality of the establishment is simply to turn up and ask to see a room. Of course, if you are booking ahead, this is not possible, so the more literature you receive and asking the right questions to the owners or management should be enough to ensure a comfortable stay.

If you **do** wish to understand the scheme, the STB and the local office (see below) have guidebooks available to let you know what to expect in their graded properties.

There is also the matter of the Ayrshire and Arran Tourist Board. This is (although not as simple as it sounds) the local area office for the Scottish Tourist Board, situated at the pier in Brodick. The Ayrshire and Arran Tourist Board was formed between the two areas several years ago (and is likely to be merged again with even larger chunk of south east Scotland). This has, as you can imagine, upset the Arran population and the island's once proud independent tourist board is no longer a single entity. Today, independent companies and small groups of hoteliers are already heading up their own tourism marketing strategies.

By the way, other ratings schemes that you may come across on Arran are more widely known and arguable more understandable than the STB's. The AA, RAC, Michelin, Egon Ronay and so on have graded their choice of properties on the island and there are, of course, independent publications which list others.

The STB and the AATB are, however, very helpful to the general tourist as far as island information is concerned. A yearly magazine (an accommodation guide, with useful contact numbers and major Arran events) is published and the local office at Brodick can usually tell you "what's on" in all the villages.

FINDING ACCOMMODATION

Camping

There are numerous campsites around the island, most offering a good level of service, with adequate provision for caravans and back-packers with tents. Many people prefer to camp in the hills, on beaches or lay-bys. Although they are seldom enforced, there are legal issues regarding land-ownership on Arran which actually mean that it is unlawful to simply camp where you like.

Youth Hostels & Lodges

Arran's main youth hostel in Lochranza (tel:830631) is a large building, popular with visitors from all over the world. It is located in a beautiful area and consequently is very busy. A smaller hostel operates in Whiting Bay (tel: 700339). Various field centres in Shiskine, Lamlash and Lochranza accommodate groups of students and other small to medium sized parties. Brodick Castle also has a new group lodge (tel 302202).

Bed & Breakfast

B & Bs are found all over the island, as much in rural areas as the village centres. Nearly all are private houses. Bed and Breakfast establishments are often booked well in advance and many owners will prefer to take bookings for more than one night. The majority of establishments have en-suite facilities and offer a hearty Scottish breakfast.

Self-Catering

Available to those who book well in advance, self catering cottages and houses make up a large proportion of Arran's tourist requirements. Some establishments are purpose-built whilst others are "second homes" or cottages within the grounds of a larger family house. Nearly all self catering units are fully serviced with modern appliances. Not all premises allow pets, smokers or even, in obscure cases, children.

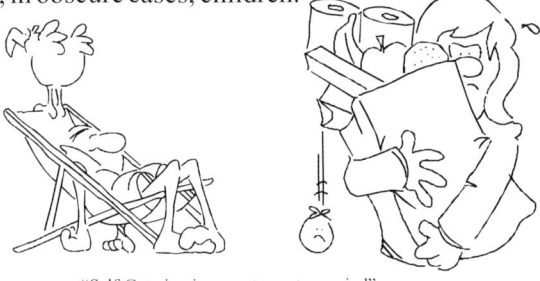

"Self-Catering is a great way to unwind"

Guest Houses and Hotels

The physical difference between a guesthouse and a hotel is not always immediately obvious. These differences usually stem from grading classifications issued by the tourist authorities (see previous section). However, it's usually a safe bet to assume that a guesthouse will mean a private home, operated by the owners, often serving an evening meal as well as breakfast. Nearly all rooms will be en-suite and a guest house will usually mean the sole source of income for the owners, so you will find more services, at a higher cost than bed and breakfast establishments. Smaller hotels are comparable to some of the larger and more established guest houses, whereas larger hotels on Arran (30 beds and over) will have meals available throughout the day, a comprehensive range of facilities and some have indoor pools and leisure areas.

ARRAN'S CLIMATE

Arran is an island in a temperate climate zone. This means that predicting weather is never easy. You will read, and hear, a lot about the "Gulf Stream" and how it affects the island. This narrow pattern of warmer winds originates in the Caribbean and is more correctly known as the "North Atlantic Drift" by the time it reaches the UK. However, I'll submit to the more romantic title of "Gulf Stream" here because, well, it sounds more atttractive! The Gulf Stream, then, wafts into the island and the surrounding area of Western Scotland and is almost imperceptibly responsible for raising the temperature by a degree or so, over the usual "mainland" forecasts. Not much, I know, but it does account for generally less snowfall in winter and the ability for locals to grow palm trees and other plants more accustomed to warmer areas. Winters, then, are cool and often damp. Storms from the Atlantic often pile into the bays creating some very good photographic opportunities for hardened visitors. However, the island also has some wonderful sunny days in winter, regardless of how cold it gets. If you do find yourself here on such a day, you'll find it hard to beat - the opportunity for a walk over frozen hills in crisp, clear air is very rewarding and the wildlife surprisingly active.

Summer temperatures often average the lower twenties Celsius, with an occasional cool sea breeze. It does rain, of course - this isn't the South Pacific. Spring and Autumn are completely unpredictable but usually have their fair share of warm sunshine and cooler, wetter days.

Visitors should not take these figures as accurate forecasts as they are taken from one year (2000).. Rather, they show the fluctuating effects of the island's weather patterns over the course of one year and the typical range of temperature on the island.

Temperatures are shown in degrees Celsius and are averages for the month in question. Arran often goes 'sub zero' in Winter.

Figures courtesy of John & Janey McLure, Brodick.

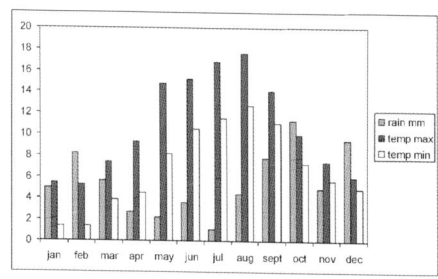

FINDING OUT "WHAT'S ON"

Local Press

The Arran Banner, the island's weekly newspaper, runs an assortment of local news, gossip and articles. Headlines and reviews often cover overly detailed investigations into a particular community activity which visitors may find incomprehensible. However, after it's columns of 'news and reviews', you may find that the back pages are more useful; containing, as they do, a handy, if brief, "what's on" guide as well as a plethora of advertisements for many of Arran's hotels, shops, restaurants and other hospitality-related businesses.

By the way, one thing that you will definitely notice about Arran as soon as you read the Banner is that the island is almost entirely "committee-run". There are committees for just about everything with many locals involved in more than half a dozen such organisations at any one time! This is not a criticism - many of Arran's committees are responsible for helping to maintain the island's 'good points' in some way - rather, it is a curiously interesting phenomenon that is only really spotted when you study the island as a distinctly enclosed area.

Posters & Boards

It's often a safe bet to find out what's going on by the almost "death-by-poster" mentality of the local business community. Almost every shop, post office, hotel and restaurant has had to make space for a "notice-board" in their foyer or front window. There is a big outdoor display of posters at Brodick Post Office and you will often find something stapled to telephone poles in the rural areas.

The Tourist Information Centre

The office at the pier in Brodick will be able to give you dates and directions for Arran's major summer events.

The Locals

If in doubt, ask a local! By far the easiest way to find out if there's anything going on in a particular village is simply to ask a local shopkeeper. There's a good possibility that he/she will be involved in local events directly and you may find out more than you expected.

Stuck for choice?

The 'problem' with local events is that they often clash in the height of the summer as committees and communities fight for the key weekends and evenings to gain maximum support from locals and visitors. It's almost unavoidable, with nearly every community running a village fair, the major events such as the Arran Highland Show, The Castle Show, sports events and music festivals. However, it's simply a matter of what you fancy doing. If the weather's good, it shouldn't matter what you choose to do. If it's raining, choose an event that at least has a marquee or hall to escape to.

When are the key weekends?

Most village fares take place in the school holidays between late June and early September. Sporting events such as the Arran Open are usually in early June, followed by the Arran Folk Festival (usually 3 - 6 days on the second week on June). The outdoor shows, agricultural events and so on are held between mid July and late August.

POPULAR ARRAN EVENTS AND (APPROX) DATES:

Brodick Castle Fair - a small country fair in the castle grounds; July
The Arran Folk Festival - an island wide celebration of Arran and International folk musicians, lots of beer drinking and late nights for all; June (2nd week)
Shiskine Sports - a range of standard and not-so-standard sports to get involved in; July
The Highland Show - plenty of bagpipes and highland games type activities in Brodick ; August
The Arran Show - the more agricultural event with added horses and dogs; August (Lamlash)
Corrie Capers - boat burning, bed racing and other strange goings-on; August
Lochranza Gala Weekend- a dubious but often amusing ~~water fight~~ boat "race", fete and dances; late July
Bonfire Night - fires and other pyromania in most villages (not always on the 5th, it can be anywhere between the 2nd and the 7th depending on weather and weekend dates - most are held on Fri or Sat nights).

Village Halls and their events

Throughout the village sections of the book you will see direct or indirect references to Arran's village halls. These are often large community venues, some of which, like Lochranza's, are brand new, thanks to funding available through the Millennium Halls project. Some halls are not used every week and visitors are often unaware that most are able to be rented for family gatherings, wedding receptions and so on - often with catering and bar options. When there is something on, it's well worth finding out more. There are local slideshows, occasional films, musical evenings (some of which are from local bands, groups or choirs and some are 'imported acts' from the mainland) and discos. To find out more, ask the local shop or try the back of the Arran Banner.

DANGEROUS PLANTS AND WILDLIFE

In most area-specific guidebooks of the world, you find references of plants to avoid and animals that, although deadly, are "probably more frightened that you are..." when encountered. Not to be outdone, here's Arran's somewhat small section of things to avoid.

Whilst there is little to worry about on the plant side, there are, indeed, animals requiring a wide berth if spotted. Adders, or Vipers, are the UK's only poisonous snakes and Arran has its' fair share. They are very dark in colour (almost black) and are found most often basking in the sun on rocks or cooling off in long grass, usually up in the hills and mountains. They are not exactly common, but you should be aware of them and avoid letting your children and/or dog anywhere near one if spotted. Red Deer are common in the north of the island and have grown accustomed to the human population. They can be a hazard on roads as much as anything else, but during their "rutting season" in late autumn the stags should not be approached whilst they are busy attracting a female partner. On the beaches during the summer you will often find jellyfish washed up. This is an indication that there are lots more in the sea. There are some varieties that will sting you. In hot summers they can be huge in size or quantity.

Lastly, on the "dangerous" list, is the Scottish Midge. Not so much "dangerous" as "frustrating", this little insect is the ruin of many a good barbecue. Midges rarely cause long lasting discomfort. Unfortunately, on occasional calm evenings in summer, particularly after a light shower, parts of the island can come alive with these almost microscopic flies which simply like to tuck into a good arm or neck for a quick bite. They are more a short-term nuisance and many people who are targets for midges simply 'last out the storm' indoors. The irritation from a midge bite rarely lasts more than an hour or so. Do not confuse midges with mosquitoes that would be like comparing a slingshot with a .45 magnum. It must be said that most visitors to Arran never witness any bad encounters with wildlife.

Before I leave this section, a word about sharks. Arran has a number of shark species that visit predominantly during the late summer season. By far the most obvious is the basking shark, the world's second biggest fish, which can grow to around 45 feet in length. They are spotted so easily because more than the large dorsal fin is visible when they are cruising around the coast. You will often see the nose of the fish, the fin and the tail, thereby giving you a rough idea of its' size. The huge and somewhat frighteningly large mouth is rarely visible unless you are in a boat but regardless of where you are when you witness a basking shark, there's little cause for alarm. These sharks eat little except microscopic plankton, so enjoy being as close as you can get and ignore the "Jaws" signature tune being hummed by people around you!

WHERE TO SEE WILDLIFE.

Seals. Grey seals are found all around the coast, but in larger numbers at Kildonan, Lamlash (the Claughland's Point area) and Lochranza (Newton Shore). You'll often see seals sunbathing on rocks in the shallow waters near the Brodick Castle entrance and towards Corrie.

Red Deer. Although they can be seen just about everywhere except the south west of the island, deer are more common and more obvious in Lochranza. You will see herds anywhere north of Corrie, especially in the hills but occasionally on or near the road. After Sannox, when you start to climb the "Boguillie" hills, you should have no problem spotting deer on the mountainsides. Once you reach the village of Lochranza, however, you can be up to your roof rack in large stags. Some deer are so close to domestication that they can be hand fed by strangers but this can be dangerous to both the deer and to people. Bad habits like this don't help keep them where the deer should be (in the hills) and many are hit by cars on the road in this area each year.

Otters. Although still uncommon, there are signs of increased otter sightings all over the island. They can be found anywhere near the shore or alongside fast flowing streams well inland. Although many people don't get to witness an otter, they can often be mistaken for young seals playing in the shallows. The best places to try to see an otter are on the eastern side of the island near Corrie, the lonely stretch of Arran's north coast (you'll need to walk there from Sannox or Lochranza) and some of the stream outlets on the east coast at Catacol Glen and further south.

Golden Eagles. What's the difference between a golden eagle and a buzzard? You'll need to know the answer to that before you've satisfied yourself of a positive sighting. There are, apparently, two pairs of eagles who reside on Arran. One pair is reportedly seen on the String Road and the other on the Boguillie, towards Lochranza. I am always under the impression that there may be more but this is possibly the annual offspring of the recognised pairs and possibly wrong sightings. Certainly, there are hundreds of buzzards on Arran as well as barn owls (Corrie), and other birds of prey (especially on Machrie Moor).

Dolphins, Porpoises and Sharks. Unfortunately, the more aquatic visitors to Arran seemingly have no preference for location around the shores. If you are in a boat, or walking on the shoreline when the sea is flat calm you can occasionally hear dolphins and porpoises long before you see them. Sharks, once they are in the area, are big and very noticeable.

Also look out for Red Squirrels, mink, small lizards, hundreds of species of birds (there is an annual Bird Report published each year on Arran available all around the island) and don't forget the plant life either - the Arran Flora is another annual book which is published locally.

LOCAL SERVICES

Postal Services on, and off, Arran.

As you will imagine, postal services on and off the island are affected by ferry sailings. Mail to the island arrives early in the day during the summer, but use of alternative methods in winter usually mean that deliveries of mail can be expected much later in the day. Obviously, most visitors only send mail to destinations off the island. Postcards and letters must be posted no later than 3.45pm in Brodick and earlier in outlying areas (see local post boxes) to be sure that they leave the island that night. There is always a risk that first class mail for the UK may not arrive "next day", so guaranteed services should be used for important letters or packages.

If you have reason to send mail within the island, note that the post office generally handles second-class mail as quickly as first class.

Arran's Telephone Numbers

All numbers that appear in this book do so without the STD (area) code. This, for the entire island, is **01770**. It is unnecessary to dial the STD code if you are on the island dialling another local number but you will need the code for dialling to the island and, of course, for your mobile phone.

Business and Communication Services.

Arran has been slow to catch up with the demands from the business traveller, but recently there have been significant changes to the services you can now receive on the island. Recognised, too, is the demand for Internet and email services and although visitors normally understand the seasonal problems with businesses like these being set up and run profitably, there are now moves to improve facilities during the season.

Internet & Email Access

At the time of going to press, Brodick Library is rumoured to be developing this service. There is also a proposed service at the new Lochranza and Catacol Village Hall and at the Auchrannie Spa Resort (see Brodick Section).

Laptop & Fax Services

If you are travelling on business and need emergency printing from your own laptop, Arran Graphics and Computers can probably help (located in the rear of "Inspirations" on the shore front in Brodick. Open Mon - Fri, 0900 - 1700, tel 302060). Be aware that prices are usually high and you will have to make an appointment. Some hotels and the two estate agents can also offer fax facilities and several of the larger establishments can usually handle business requirements in addition to this.

Photocopying

Black & white photocopying is available at Arran Estate Agents (on the seafront in Brodick) and Alldays supermarket, Brodick. Colour photocopying is available at "Motto Plaks" just alongside the second tee of Brodick Golf Course on the main road.

Mobile Phone Reception

Generally, the signal strength for cell-phones is adequate around the island. Several black spots, especially in the mountain areas and occasional reports in Whiting Bay and the Cladach area of Brodick can still cause disruption to signals. It's often the case that different systems can achieve different results, of course, but the top providers, including Orange, Cellnet and Vodafone, seem to have Arran pretty much covered.

Mobile Phone vouchers

For those with cell-phones which require pre-paid vouchers, a good range is available from Brodick Post Office.

Photographic Film Developing

Services exist at the Chemists, Brodick (tel 302250) and the shop can offer same-day services and one-hour services if required, especially for those requiring emergency processing.

Passport Photographs

A new and somewhat amusing (but functional) photo booth has been installed in Brodick Post Office.

Laundry

You can 'do your own' laundry at the Good Food Shop (okay, so it's next door!) in Brodick at their tiny coin-operated laundrette. Larger hotels will, of course, offer a service where possible. A dry cleaning laundry service is carried out by the Gift Shop and Boutique, Brodick (likely to be renamed "Bilsland's" by the time this book goes to press. This is usually a 3 or 4 day service.

Veterinary

If your animal needs the service of a veterinary surgeon, a daily service is operated just behind the Royal Bank of Scotland in Brodick. Malcolm Wheeler runs surgery hours most weekday mornings. Don't book, just turn up.

Interflora / Flowers

If you need flowers for a wedding or funeral, try Brodick Nursery Gardens, opposite the pier junction in Brodick. Tel: 302684.

Newspaper Advertising

The Arran Banner is the island's only newspaper, available every Saturday (45p). They run private advertisements as well as public notices. The Arran Banner is located next door to the Douglas Hotel in Brodick (tel: 302142)

Local Council

The local council offices are located (most of them) in Lamlash, just a few yards along the road towards the hospital. Their main switchboard number is 01770 600338

Housing

Arran is one of the first areas of Scotland to have an independent housing company in charge of what used to be termed the 'council houses'. *Isle of Arran Homes* was set up in 2001 and now runs and maintains all 'community housing' on the island. Their number is 01770 303700.

Estate Agents

Now you've seen the island, what's to stop you living here?! Try Arran Estate Agents on the shore road in Brodick (tel: 302310) or Brodick Estate Agents on 302017. Both have listings of the majority of property for sale.

THE ISLAND OF ARRAN GUIDEBOOK

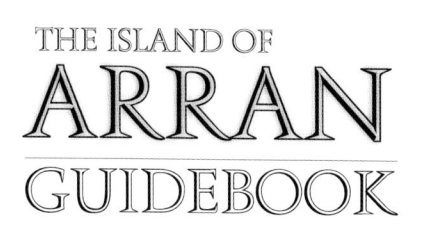

THE VILLAGES

"Watch for low-flying golf balls!"

This section describes the villages in greater detail. The descriptions of larger villages follow a route through the village (this is usually east to west or 'away from Brodick'), giving the visitor an indication of the location of the place they may be looking for. Maps relating to the larger villages are towards the end of the book.

Telephone numbers have been given. Don't forget Arran's STD dialling code is 01770 if you are dialling from the mainland (drop the leading '0' if you are calling from overseas. The CD Rom, as mentioned, has more contact details by way of web sites.

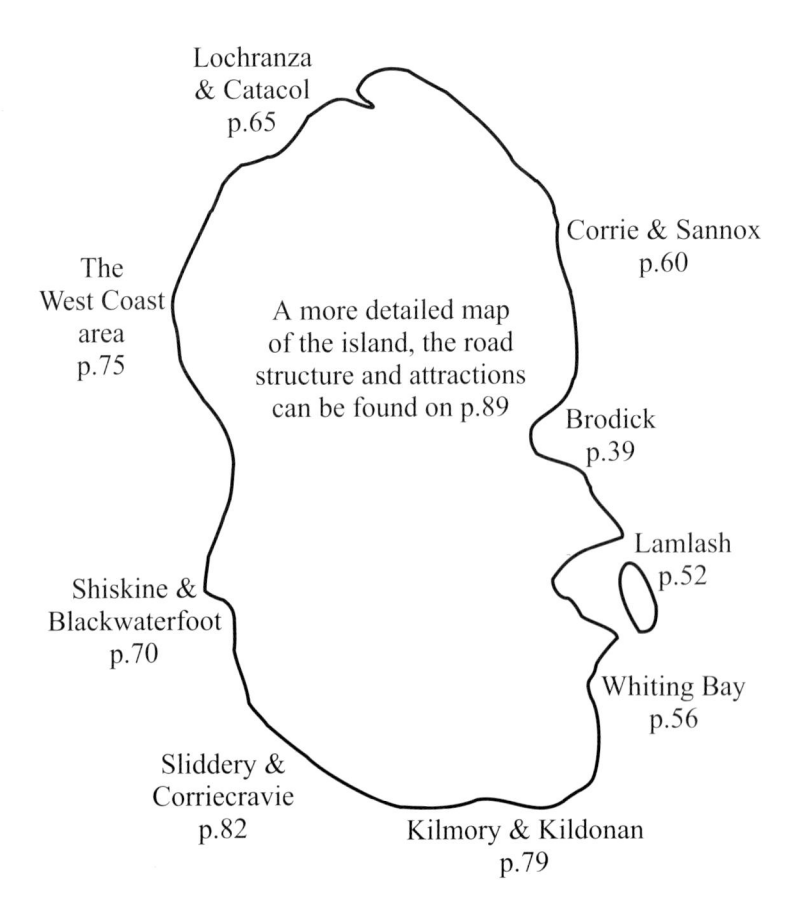

Lochranza
& Catacol
p.65

Corrie & Sannox
p.60

The
West Coast
area
p.75

A more detailed map of the island, the road structure and attractions can be found on p.89

Brodick
p.39

Lamlash
p.52

Shiskine &
Blackwaterfoot
p.70

Whiting Bay
p.56

Sliddery &
Corriecravie
p.82

Kilmory & Kildonan
p.79

BRODICK

Brodick stretches around the large open bay on the mid-eastern side of the island. Often perceived as the "capital" of the island (although Lamlash has, historically, more right to the title), Brodick is usually the busiest area on Arran. Almost all commercial activity has to operate through this small village of just over 1,000 inhabitants. The main road through the village passes the majority of the shops and businesses along the shorefront.

Brodick's East End

The "pier end" of Brodick is dominated by ferry-related activity all year. Squeezed into this small pocket of space at the southeast side of the village is both the ferry terminal and the main bus "station". Also crammed in here is access (via Market Road) to busy commercial operations such Arran Deliveries (couriers), Arran Dairies (makers of the new range of Arran ice cream which is available all around the island) and Arran's only 24-hour breakdown service, Angus Lambie Motor Engineers (tel; 302677). Market Road - a no-through road - is possibly Arran's worst stretch of public road. In fact, the tarmac runs out very quickly and is replaced by a dusty potholed track that makes you appreciate the repair garage at the end even more! Don't come down here unless you are visiting the garage.

Caledonian MacBrayne's terminal is a pleasant low-level building set at the pier head and is the only place to buy tickets for the Brodick to Ardrossan run if you haven't already booked. There is a large holding area here for ferry traffic but if you are not travelling, you are best parking along the shorefront further in towards the village. The small car park at the Tourist Information Centre is often congested when ferry sailings are due to depart and the whole area is swamped with buses, trucks, cars and pedestrians during these short periods of time, about 4 or 5 times a day. There are petrol facilities here, courtesy of Arran Transport, as well as several shops within the "pier buildings" complex. A fish and chip shop, The Ferry Fry, was Brodick's only dedicated take-away restaurant until the more recent Chinese Restaurant opened in the centre of the village

The Tourist Information Centre is open daily throughout the season (tel: 302140) and is operated by The Ayrshire and Arran Tourist Board. There is local information on most events, a range of leaflets from businesses on Arran (and from Ayrshire) and an accommodation booking service. Note that the majority of accommodation business conducted through the Tourist Information Centre will favour its members.

The junction onto the main road at this point will take you either south towards Lamlash, Whiting Bay and Kildonan or through the village of Brodick and then towards a further junction for Blackwaterfoot (west) or Corrie and Lochranza in the north.

Situated just south of the pier buildings, past Brodick Nursery Gardens, is the small "hamlet" of Corriegills. These well-established and often large houses overlook the bay towards the castle and are mostly residential. Further down the Corriegills road, Henry Murdo's Bagpipe workshop produces bagpipes of International quality. This workshop is not open for the public, but you can contact Henry through his website at www.arransites.co.uk.

Travelling right at the pier junction, the road travels through the centre of the village. Large hotels and the Co-op supermarket dominate this stretch of road, but there are also some smaller shopping areas, such as the Douglas Centre. Here, you'll find Arran's only Opticians (McAlister's tel: 302878), the interestingly names "Arran Asia Trading Company", who deal in clothes and other - mostly textile - goods from the far east, the Arran Sweetie Kitchen and a hairdressers. Opposite the Douglas Centre, tucked under the trees, is the 'Arran Banner' office. Arran's weekly newspaper is printed here and is available widely throughout the island every Saturday.

The Co-op, which moved from its old store in the heart of the village, is now the largest supermarket (and the largest retailer) on Arran. Provisions and groceries are aimed more towards the "necessity" items and you are more likely to find unusual or exotic food items at "Alldays" or "The Good Food Shop".

Opposite the Co-op is the newly constructed slipway for the launching of small boats and for tenders of larger yachts and cruisers. This is a huge benefit to both visiting yachts and those with their own boat trailers on the island. There is adequate space to turn a car and trailer and these can be parked, if necessary, in the adjacent shore road parking spaces, with care. Out into the bay, visiting yachts-people will note that there are provisions for safe anchorages during the summer. These blue bouys are anchored every year and are available to visitors on a first-come, first-served basis.

Brodick's Gift Shop & Boutique is heading for a major facelift in the near future and has just, on the very day this book went to press, been demolished! The new giftshop which will be called "Bilsland's" will continue to have one of the largest selections of everyday clothing on the island and promises to improve on it's range of goods in general . Naturally, gifts are available in all shapes and sizes and there are toys and games for the children.

The Shore & Bay

Note that the natural bay at Brodick is not as protected as Lamlash (headquarters of the Arran Yacht Club). Brodick Bay often becomes very rough in easterly winds and there have been numerous occasions of yachts being stranded on the beaches after dragging their anchors.

On the subject of beaches, the broad bay of Brodick is one of the largest stretches of relatively safe sandy beach on the island. Backing on to the golf course and the low-lying areas of marshland between, the beach curves from the heart of the village to the pedestrian entrance of Brodick Castle. Recent winter storms have changed the shape of the beach, particularly near the outflow of Rosa Burn, and many different sand dunes appear in this area from time to time. Therefore, it's not always as easy as you think to walk the entire stretch of beach and a careful excursion along the public footpath on the golf course may be required.

Brodick - 'downtown'

Back in town, many of the village shops, banks and post office fit into a very small central "downtown" area. The two banks (The Royal Bank of Scotland (tel: 302222) and The Bank of Scotland (tel: [local] 892000) are the only banks on the island apart from girobank services at the post office (tel: 302245). Banking facilities include bureau de change (from foreign currency to sterling only, unless you can wait 48 hours) and international services. Both banks also have cash (ATM) machines operating 24 hours a day. Bank vans travel the island to help residents and visitors from coming in to Brodick. Timetables are available from the bank tellers.

Between the Royal Bank of Scotland and Brodick Golf Club, the village's "downtown" area is packed with gift shops, grocery stores, Arran's main bakery, the Bank of Scotland (24 hr-ATM) and the central Post Office, which is open daily (exc Sunday) see "mail". Arran has two island-based Estate Agents which are both located in this area of Brodick . Arran Estate Agents (tel: 302310) is just a few doors down from Brodick Estate Agents (tel: 302017) next-door to the largest bookshop on the island, the Book and Card Centre. Just along from this is the new Arran Chocolate Factory (tel: 302873) which makes a very wide range of filled chocolates, truffles and so on. You can watch through a small window as the rich liquid chocolate continually flows through one machine into a large vat. There are often 'tasters' on the counter.

Within this often-busy area of Brodick, you could do worse than stop off at the Brodick Bar and Brassiere for a lunch break or evening meal. Alldays grocery store was, and maybe still is, in direct competition with the Co-op, just 800 yards up the road. But Alldays (tel: 302212) specialise in more delicatessen items, along with the usual necessities. They are also the island's largest newspaper and magazine retailers, video-hire specialists and they have a good selection of wines and beers. You can also purchase National Lottery tickets here, as well as in the aforementioned Co-op. The car park for Alldays is often chaotic, but it's the most central. Here, too, is the only place you'll find LPG gas on the island incorporated in one of the two petrol stations in Brodick (the other being at the pier). Petrol here is available from 8.30am till around 5.30pm daily, with restricted Sunday hours. Sadly, there is no compressed air service here, a facility that is now lacking in the village and only available at repair garages. Petrol is available in 4-star and unleaded (premium grade, '95' RON only); plus diesel.

Alongside Alldays, a large beach hut stocks toys, fishing tackle and souvenirs as well as beachwear. Also here you'll find cycle hire and a good putting green (all equipment is hired by the Beach Hut). The Boathouse (tel: 302868) remains one of the only places on Arran to hire fishing boats on the island. These are fully equipped with motors, life jackets and you can hire tackle. Don't expect to catch much more than mackerel but, even so, it's a fun day out.

Over the road, Inspirations of Arran is one of Arran's largest gift shops and stocks local books, produce from Paterson Arran, The Island Cheese Co and Walkers of Scotland as well as an interesting selection of aromatherapy and body care products. You can book aromatherapy, massage, or reiki sessions here with Jan Attkins, one of Arran's qualified therapists. In the back of Inspirations is Arran Graphics - an independent design company handling the majority of commercial printing on the island.

Next door to "Inspirations" stands the busy "Wooleys of Arran" bakery. (tel 302280). Wooleys are best known for their Oatcakes, now sold all over Scotland, but they are also locally known for their rolls, bloomers and large selection of sandwiches and cakes. Lately, the bakery has also been stocking Arran Ice Cream. The bakery is open 7 days a week in the summer, from early morning until 5pm. The Bank of Scotland (open usual banking hours, with 24-hr ATM) stands next door to a small row of shops including Kames Antiques (retailers of antiques, modern china, porcelain, watches and so on) and Arran's only Chinese Take-away, The Shanghai.

Around the corner from the Shanghai, the main Post Office is a formidable, if slightly ungainly, collection of buildings just off the main road. The post office itself is a small portion of the main buildings and includes a well-stocked gift shop (with a wide range of greetings cards) and the island's only instant "photo-booth". The post office is open every day excluding Sunday and closes early on Saturdays (around 12.45).

Leaving the shops of Brodick, passing the hall and library (you can hire the tennis courts behind the hall), the new sports pavilion and golf club live opposite each other and account for a large amount of Arran's sports facilities. There is also a lawn bowling club here, hidden behind the high hedges near the golf club. The new pavilion, with running track and football/rugby facilities is used not only for sporting events but also acts as a showground for various events in the summer (parking at these can be a nightmare and you are better off leaving your car back along the shorefront). Brodick Golf Club is one of Arran's most popular and holds the annual Arran Open. Although you can't rent clubs here, there is a well-stocked Pro Shop run by professional golfer, Peter McCalla. (tel: 302513).

Just around the sharp bend in the road, the Good Food Shop (tel: 302427) sells delicatessen items, fresh fish and vegetarian specialities as well as having a small tearoom in the rear. There is also a coin-operated laundry here, operated by the aforementioned Good Food Shop.

"You'll find fresh fish at the Good Food Shop"

The Auchrannie Spa Resort

Following several years of planning, cancellations, re-negotiations and debate, Arran's largest individual tourism development for some years has now been completed.

The resort sits across from the older Auchrannie Hotel and Leisure Club, still very much in operation. The entrance, however, is now a little further down the road past the golf clubhouse, at a small junction where "Motto Plaks" shop is located. A couple of hundred yards down this narrow road, the huge buildings come into view and you immediately realise the extent of the facility.

The resort, the brainchild of Auchrannie owner Iain Johnston, has been a huge undertaking, especially for Arran. The £5m or so that has been quoted for its construction is certainly visible and the decor, furnishings and labyrinth of indoor rooms and corridors are very tastefully finished.

Inside, there are hotel rooms (expect modern, travel-lodge type accommodation with just a hint of more luxurious fittings and decor), a gymnasium, a large and attractive pool area with drinks bar, a cafeteria-bar used from breakfast to dinner-time, several conference rooms, a games room for children, a (big) 'sports hall', a large shop and other leisure facilities that one might expect from such a facility. Although the building was still being completed as this book went to press, there are plans for an Internet café as well. These facilities are very much open for all - the hotel bedrooms being let on a "room-only" basis.

The whole building, put simply, is a stunning achievement and a big venue like this can service a lot of people, comfortably, on days when the weather is not great. The accommodation is the most modern on the island and will be recognisable as a worldwide standard in a hotel of this type. There is no doubt, therefore, that the resort will be a popular place to visit for visitors of all ages, including business-people who are coming to Arran for meetings, or other corporate events.

However, where the resort wins on its new squeaky-clean image and it's range of services and facilities, it loses out on the very thing that may have brought you to Arran. There are no sea views, just the valleys of "Glencloy" and there is little authentic local charm that you'd find in other places to stay. You may feel out-of-place walking through the business-like reception area with backpack and walking boots and the facilities inside may keep you from exploring or visiting other villages. There is also the 'risk' that it may tempt the children away from the great outdoors for too long.

Used as a rainy-day treat, an evening rendezvous, a place to tone the muscles or a place to do business, the Auchrannie Spa Resort is ideal - and barely challenged on the island. In winter it will certainly be well-used by the local population. Just don't forget the rest of Arran!

North Brodick & Cladach.

The Arran Heritage Museum (tel: 302636) with it's somewhat tricky car park, lies just short of the main junction to the western part of the island. The rather quaint buildings house many relics and artefacts, displays of the old crafting communities and an insight into what the island was like in the past. There is a small tearoom, the Rosaburn Café, in the rear of the building.

Situated just outside the village on the north road towards the castle, the Duchess Court Shops area has a large selection of themed gift shops and is located alongside the factory shop and visitor centre of Arran Aromatics, the island's leading employer and exporter of body care products and, lately, candles. It's another of those places to enjoy if the weather is not quite warm and dry enough and the viewing windows are helpful if you wish to see how certain products are made. There's a small café in the main shopping area. Creelers Seafood Restaurant and Smokehouse is located here (smokehouse tel: 302797; restaurant tel: 302810) as well as the Island Cheese Company where both imported and home-made cheeses are sold (tel: 302788). Do not confuse this cheese company with the other one at Kilmory, who make the Arran Dunlop variety. Behind this collection of shops is Arran Haulage - the island's main hauliers, who also supply the island with Calor gas, barbecues and, somewhat obscurely, horse-riding gear and pet food. Who said the island wasn't diverse?!

Just up the road about 400 yards lies the small hamlet of Cladach. No residential houses are here now, but a new visitor centre has been made up from the recent developments in the area. Cladach is now becoming very popular, not least because of the building of the custom-design micro brewery (tel: 302353). You can call in here for a sample of their award-winning beer, learn about how it is made and walk past the various vats of fermenting hops on a self-guided 'tour'. The beer comes out in three distinct varieties; Arran Blonde won "Champion Wheat Beer of Britain" in 2000 and it's a strong, 5%, golden coloured beer with a very pronounced flavour. The others, Arran Light and Arran Dark are less strong, and cater for individual tastes. All the beers come in large bottles, but are also available throughout the island and Scotland in pubs as draft beers.

The Wineport restaurant is located here, in Cladach (see eating out), and also the recently relocated outfitters, Arran Active (tel: 302416). Arran Active, which sells walking poles, fleeces, jackets, boots and camping equipment amongst other things, is ideally situated for the start of the most popular track up to Goatfell, Arran's highest peak (see section below), which is opposite the shop. Mackenzie Leather also has their shop here and although most of their articles such as bags and cases are destined for retailers on the mainland, they have a small number of samples on display.

Crucial to the development of this area is the pedestrian entrance to Brodick Castle. This is a new entrance, relocated from further up the main road and means that not only buses find it easier to drop passengers off here, but also several large car parks cater for the busiest of weekends. You can walk here from Brodick, using the beach paths and a new bridge just opposite the Cladach Centre. Drivers should note, however, that no charge is made for parking or, indeed, taking a car into the castle grounds and substantial car parking space is available just inside the main visitor entrance further up the road. Visitors, however, should not use this as a free car park without using the facilities of the castle. There are fuller details on the castle on page 49.

Goatfell

Arran's highest peak, at 2866 feet, is perhaps not as awe-inspiring as the jagged and seemingly higher peaks of the mountains to the east, but it does mean that you can climb up and down Goatfell relatively easily in around 5 hours. Children as young as four have been known to make the trip. If the weather suits, it's best to reserve most of the day to the mountain, pack a lunch and follow the well-marked trail from Brodick to the summit. After the initial walk through the forest, the trail leads onto the moorland and crosses the stream at an attractive bridge around half way up. Once you've reached the ridge (not by any means dangerous unless you walk too far off the trail to the north), you are greeted by the fact that, all of a sudden, the trail disintegrates under a large amount of loose boulders which, to most, is the most gruelling part of the climb. By this point you are so close to the summit not to worry about the odd aching joint and once you reach the top, the views to Ireland, the Hebrides and the west coast of Scotland are quite something (apparently). Having done the trip twice myself, I still wait for the day that I can climb the thing before the mist comes in! Needless to say, choose a good sunny day and take lightweight wet-weather protection - weather on Arran can change in minutes. Attempting to return on a different route is possible (you can try coming back down to Corrie, but bear in mind that the ridges and peaks on Arran are precipitous. The Brodick route to Goatfell is, however, one of the safest long walks on Arran and you simply must do it if you have the time.

"Don't underestimate the severity of Arran's mountain ridges!"

Brodick Castle, Gardens and Country Park.

Perhaps the most renowned man-made attraction on Arran, Brodick Castle (tel; 302202) and its impressive gardens are on the agenda for many people who come to Arran for the day or longer.

The entrance to Brodick Castle is on a tight bend just a few hundred yards after the Cladach Centre. Drive through the formidable gateway and into the main car parking area but note that this is all one-way (the exit is about half a mile down the main road nearer Brodick) so you should arrange to pick anyone up at the visitor centre rather than the somewhat dangerously located main entrance. If you are disabled or require any assistance in getting to the castle from the car park (there are a few steps to climb) the National Trust has an electric 'minibus' service available.

The main reception area and shop is an attractive and well-stocked building, with a new "plant sales" area should visitors wish to try growing Arran-grown seedlings at home.

Owned by the National Trust for Scotland, the castle is one of Scotland's most impressive both externally and internally. Self-guided tours of the interior rooms (there are volunteer guides who are on call in most of the rooms) are worth taking to see how the castle was changed over time and with various occupants. Lavish furnishings, decoration and a magnificent trophy collection (we're talking stags heads here, so vegetarians beware) add to the distinctly authentic Scottish feel. A tearoom, with seating outside overlooking the bay, is a popular and often manically busy area (coach parties often visit the castle in mid season).

The gardens, as well known as the castle, are abundant with rhododendron and other more unusual and exotic plants and trees. Nigel Price (the head gardener) and his team have stunning collections of shrubs and flowers from all over the world, especially China, where many of the rhododendrons originate. Tall Eucalyptus trees grow next to California Redwoods giving a weird, but interesting combination of mature woodland species.

continued...

Before you worry about deforestation within the gardens (there are many signs of felled trees) you should note that a major storm on Arran in the late 1990's brought thousands of trees down in the gardens and, more predominantly, in the surrounding forest park. Some of these areas have been cleared and other areas are being replanted.

Within the garden walkways you will find an interesting summerhouse and an icehouse is hidden away on one of the trails. Perhaps not exciting enough for the children, they get their opportunity in the castle's grounds where a large adventure playground sits just away from the Ranger centre (a small display room is open to show the wildlife and habitat of the area).

Away from the castle and it's gardens, the land is taken over by the Forest Enterprise and several smaller marked routes take you on circular walks around the area, always returning to the central car park or Ranger centre. These walks are well illustrated on the castle's leaflets.

The exit to the castle is some distance from the entrance (almost back at the junction with the "String road"). This exit road from the car park is one-way only.

Eating out in Brodick

A popular brasserie, The Brodick Bar (tel: 302169), located opposite the post office serves excellent bar meals in newly refurbished surroundings and has a good selection of draft beers on tap. Duncan's Bar (tel: 302531) on the shore road (and part of the Kingsley Hotel) also serves good bar food and has a beer garden overlooking the bay. Others pubs serving food include the Ormidale (tel: 302293), behind the sports pavilion on Knowe Road, which is often busy with folk musicians and other local acts. At Cladach, the relatively new Wineport Bistro, which was closed in late season 2001, has hopefully reopened since this book went to press.
You can also book dinner at the Auchrannie Hotel / Spa Resort in any of their restaurants (tel: 302234) or just turn up during any part of the day for coffee or snacks in either building. Just outside Brodick on the shore road to Corrie, the popular "Pirates Cove" restaurant can be booked for evening meals (tel:

302438). Brodick Castle's 'restaurant' (tel: 302202) offers coffees, afternoon teas and other light snacks, and the less expensive but just as popular Rosaburn Café at the Heritage Museum in Brodick also serves food throughout the day.

Take-away food is available in the shape of fish and chips (amongst other things) from The Ferry Fry at the pier (tel: 302656) and the Chinese restaurant, The Shanghai, in the downtown area of Brodick near the post office (tel: 303777), is open every day except Wednesdays for take-out oriental cuisine.

Overnight in Brodick

A campsite at Glen Rosa just off the String Road at the northern end of Brodick is a fair walk from the pier, but it's the closest site for camping if you're just off the ferry. Camping on the grassland between the shore and the golf course in Brodick is not only discouraged but can be dangerous as this stretch of land often floods at high tide or during stormy weather. For a roof over your head, at the lower end of the price range, The Allandale Hotel (tel: 302278), Connemara (tel: 302488), Strathwhillan Lodge (tel: 302331) and Tigh-na-Mara (tel 302538) all offer similar services and pleasant, functional rooms. The Invercloy (tel: 302225), in the centre of the village, has been extensively redecorated inside and has good views of Brodick Bay from some rooms. The Belvedere Guest House (tel: 302397) on Alma Road has even more impressive views and, as well as catering for the general visitor, offers relaxing themed breaks. Kilmichael Country House Hotel (tel: 302219) is the island's most luxuriously appointed hotel and sits in tranquil gardens at the end of Knowe Road. The new Auchrannie Spa Resort complex now adds over 30 rooms and more amenities to an already large and well-established hotel in the Glencloy area of Brodick (not visible from the road). The Auchrannie also has RCI timeshare lodges, an indoor pool and a leisure/gym complex. (tel main reception: 302234). The Kingsley (tel: 302226) has a pool, bar and pleasant sun lounge. It caters for groups as well as individuals and families. There are, of course, many other establishments in Brodick including bed and breakfast and self-catering units which are found throughout the village. A booking agency for self catering units, run by Arran Holiday Properties (tel: 302303), is located at Arran Estate Agents in the heart of the village.

LAMLASH

Lamlash is a village that clings on to its historical roots as the former capital of the island. The basis for the title was founded on the fishing, shipping and ferry traffic that used Lamlash and it's wide, safe harbour. These days, of course, the ships have gone and have been replaced by a large flotilla of anchored yachts and cruisers that benefit from the same security in the bay.

The village still has key features that are not found in Brodick. The Arran High School is located in Lamlash as is the main hospital, police station and fire station. The shops and businesses are not as obvious in size, or number, but the village is still very much a tourism destination, possibly because of this lack of recent development. It is also every bit as scenic as Brodick because protecting the bay is Holy Island, now home to a Buddhist monastery, which adds something rather different to the horizon. Also, the pier is accessible to the public, there being a much shallower sea-bed here which effectively rules out the possibility for modern-day ships to use such a facility.

Your approach to Lamlash from Brodick includes probably the straightest bit of road on the island, albeit less than half a mile. At the top of the road there are two Forestry Commission car parks, one with a few picnic tables, and both look out through the trees to the goatfell mountains. It's a good place to walk if it's windy, as the tall pine trees offer good shelter and there is a chance of tracing an old pathway, still marked on maps, to Brodick. This area of dense forestry is often interrupted by huge swathes of felled areas where the trees have been harvested. Although unsightly, there is evidence that replanting swiftly follows the harvest and the deforestation therefore is really only part of the cycle.

Past these areas you quickly descend to Lamlash, passing by the large and relatively new Lamlash Golf Course clubhouse. The club (tel: 600296) is one of Arran's '18-holers' and its undulating fairways are popular with locals and visitors. At the foot of the hill is a junction which takes you right, towards the village or, towards (and hopefully not 'to') the hospital, which is out of sight behind the first row of beach-front houses. If you do turn down here, keep going down the shore road and you'll find yourself at Claughland's Point which is a good place to see grey seals and to photograph Holy Isle.

Back on the main road, and taking a right turn at the shore, the heart of Lamlash village comes into view. It's a narrow road through some parts, often busy, but there are a number of small car parks between the shops and restaurants. Like Brodick, the village skirts around the sweeping bay, with most residential houses located back off the road or on the hillsides, leaving the main road to be occupied by retailers, hotels and other businesses.

The Lamlash Store is a well presented village shop selling newspapers, ice cream, beer, wine, spirits, groceries and so on. They share a car park with the Drift Inn, hidden 'round the back' with excellent views and outdoor seating. This pleasant public house serves food throughout the day. A bowling green is also in this small area of the village.

Lamlash postal services are not as expansive as those in Brodick, but stamps and basic postal requirements are offered (tel: 600201).

A sport shop, R & R Sports is next door to Studio 4 - a small art gallery which has local arts and crafts for sale.. Crawford and Barbour (tel: 600294) have a video library.

The pier and surrounding area is a common boating area - there is usually a lot of activity around here and Arran's only chandlery, Johnston's Marine Stores (tel: 600333) is located just at the head of the pier. This is a handy place for any nautical equipment you may require, including ropes, fastenings and other supplies. The shop also sells fishing tackle, Seagull engine parts, maps and clothing. The main lifeboat station on Arran also has a new building here, just next to the pier. Should you fancy taking the trip over to Holy Isle (now owned by Buddhist monks) you can book ferry trips at the caravan on the pier head. The fares are around £8 (£4 for children). The operator also runs mackerel fishing trips and supplies tackle and bait.

Along the shore front of the village a concerted effort has gone into maintaining a long grassed area with swings and the occasional bench. This is a popular place on really warm days and with picnic potential and good views of the bay, you could find yourself "chilling out" for hours as the children play on the relatively safe, but not entirely sandy, beach.

There is a pharmacy in the centre of the village (tel: 600275) and Gordon Brothers at Ship House (tel: 600231) sell an interesting range of groceries and goods, many of which are local. Arran Candlemakers (tel: 600917) also operate in Lamlash and have a wide range of distinctly unusual candles, made on the premises. The Co-op have a smaller (much smaller) version of their Brodick store further along in the village, towards the school.

There is a surgery held at the Lamlash Medical Centre which is almost opposite the High school and just along from Millers Butcher who supply a comprehensive range of fresh and frozen products.

Arran's small police station is located here (although this is not always manned as call-outs and routine island checks often mean that the entire police force are elsewhere). The police vehicles on Arran are mostly Land-Rovers due to the often tricky circumstances and general conditions that they find themselves in. If you do see a larger, more customary police car it is likely to be a mainland vehicle. These officers visit Arran routinely, especially when there are busier events being held or to join a local operation in checking private vehicles, speed (radar) exercises and so on. The local opinion on the state of Arran's roads does not mean an escape from paying the same tax as anyone else in the UK!

Just over the small humpbacked bridge towards the southern residential end of the village lies the area known as Cordon. Down this side road is Middleton Caravan and Camping Site, one of Arran's largest camping areas.

Towards Whiting Bay and at the junction of the Ross Road is one of Arran's most famous visitor attractions, the formerly known Arran Mustard Factory, which has (or still is) operating under the strangely confusing names of Paterson Arran, Arran Provisions and Arran Fine Foods (tel: 600606). There is a well-stocked shop here and you can find a wide range of Arran-made jams, preserves, mustard and pickle as well as other gifts. The setting here is very pleasant and if you have time you should venture up the Ross road. Views to Holy Isle are very scenic and the area is virtually untouched by recent tourism development. The road (to Sliddery) is about 8 miles and you can use it as a short cut to Blackwaterfoot. As mentioned earlier the Ross Road has passing places in most areas. As a small point of interest, the TV drama 'The Missing Postman', with James Bolam, was partly filmed on this stretch of road. (Arran is often used as a venue for such productions because of it's typical Scottish natural assets and the fact that it's close to Glasgow and therefore easier to get film crews to.

Eating Out in Lamlash

A small tearoom, appropriately named "Caddies" is located at the golf course and is open for snacks and light meals. In the village, the Drift Inn (tel: 600656) is very popular, not least for it's location. The Pierhead Tavern (tel: 600380), very 'public house' in it's atmosphere and decor also serves food and has tables outside, although close to the road. The Glenisle restaurant (at the Glenisle Hotel - tel: 600559) is a better place for families or couples wanting a more relaxed indoor atmosphere.

Overnight in Lamlash

Lamlash lacks the larger and more modern hotels of the sort you would find in Brodick, but still maintains to have some small, friendly establishments. The Glenisle Hotel (tel: 600559) sits right on the shore road with good views of the bay and offers facilities for children as well as a comprehensive dinner menu. Both Marine House Hotel (tel: 600298) and the Lilybank Guest House (tel: 600230) also share good views to the south.

Lamlash is a good place for sea fishing

WHITING BAY

Out of the largest three villages on Arran , Whiting Bay is by far the quieter, both in amount of traffic passing through it and by the number of facilities and tourism-based activities the village is able to host. However, it also has one of the largest number of hotels in one area, testament to the fact that regardless of it's distance from many of the modern-day attractions, the village is still preferred by many, over the busier shore roads of Brodick and Lamlash.

The road to Whiting Bay from Lamlash has been improved greatly in the last few years and the pleasant drive of around three miles leaves the coast and runs though some farmland higher on the hills, giving a good view of Holy Island and the western coast of Scotland. As you approach the village, a detour can be made to 'Kings Cross', a small hamlet with scenic beaches and picnic areas, somewhat different from it's counterpart in central London that shares the same name! Back on the main road, just before you arrive at Whiting Bay's 'city limits', a large complex of greenhouses and fruit vines gives you another taste of Arran's diversity. 'Kirkend Nursery' supplies stunning strawberries, raspberries, blackcurrants and other fruits in the season and you can buy these here, at the nursery, or in many of the village shops around the island. A pick-your-own facility is also offered for certain crops. Just at the start of the houses a small cart track takes you on a walk to Auchencairn and Knockenkelly.

A small village green sits opposite the Whiting Bay Garage (tel: 700345) and you can get petrol here. Bay Stores (tel: 700229), one of the village shops, is next door and it supplies the usual range of necessary grocery items and some gifts ideas. The range of hotels here - Argentine, Invermay, Burlington and Cameronia make up a colourful row of buildings, each offering a slightly different approach in decor. There are usually some flags flying in the front gardens as well as signs indicating that several of the hoteliers have the ability to speak more than one language.

Whiting Bay is, as most, a shore-based village sharing that peculiarity on Arran that almost all the hotels have the main road between them and the shore. The village is fairly straight in geographical terms and, despite the word 'Bay' in the village's name, the beaches of sand and stone are very much more open to the waves.

Back in the centre of the village, there's the usual variety of shops, essential village stores including The Village Shop - (tel: 700349) and a small post office (tel: 700205). Whiting Bay Hires offer a limited boat/angling hire facility (tel: 700382). Another handy shop, Bay News, not only supplies newspapers but also a range of books, fishing tackle and local maps. (tel: 700481). The larger collection of green-canopied shops on the shore side of the road belong to M.B.S. who have a comprehensive selection of home improvement materials as well as building and timber supplies. Petrol is also available here. You can park on the other side of the road in a somewhat angled car park and take a walk up to 'Crafts of Arran' - a scandinavian-type building in appearance that wouldn't look out of place in a ski resort. A wide range of local crafts is on sale as well and you can get ice-cream here to enjoy on the picnic tables outside the shop. More Arran businesses such as Skotprint and Goatley's (interior designers/kitchen installations) are located here..

Whiting Bay has a curiously large number of building suppliers, joinery services and other household maintenance providers. Throughout Arran, in fact, it would not surprise me to discover that the percentage of builders and joiners on the island per head of the population would work out similar to the number of lawyers per Americans living in Los Angeles! Maybe on the re-print I'll have that worked out and use it as a footnote! However, it's a valid point to make in that building services on Arran are alive and well - both for renovations and for new development ; and it's also rewarding to see investors on the island that generally make use of as much local talent as they can. However, I'm getting sidetracked...

The Belford Mill (tel: 700293), just off the main road at the 'Coffee Pot' tearoom, is good place to stock up on extra bedding if you have forgotten any for your self-catering unit. They also sell a wide range of other fabric and textile-related merchandise.

A small pharmacy is located in the southern area of the village (tel 700584), a few hundred yards further south from the main car park and post office area.

Whiting Bay's biggest attraction is the walk to Glenashdale Falls and Giant's Graves. Glenashdale is a relatively high waterfall for Arran and obviously at it's best after good rainfall. There's a small car park (and more space is found up the road) with a signpost and information board relating to the walk. It's a pleasant, undulating trail through grass and woodland and it goes on the list as one of Arran's best walks - the opportunity to take a long-exposure shot of the waterfall through the forest is welcomed by many people and well-worth the two hours or so that the walk will entail. The trail to Glenashdale Falls seems to terminate at the top of the waterfall (keep an eye on the kids here as it can be slippery) but you can return through the forest on the other side of the falls and the track leads down to the road, close to the golf course. To return to the road, you could retrace your steps, or walk across the top of the stream and through the woods back down to the village. The Giant's Graves are not as stunning as you would expect and are merely piles of stone surrounding a 'grave site'. There is, of course, more history to it than that but the area simply holds little of interest and it's probably better to read about the myths and legends relating to this type of non-event, especially when the waterfalls, in this case, are more attractive and interesting to look at.

The aforementioned golf course (invisible from the main road) is located away from the shore and behind most of the houses. There's a well-marked side road to the course, well-marked in that it's called Golf Course Road! The course itself (tel: 700775) is pleasant and rarely too busy although, as usual, call ahead for tee times.

The whole beachfront along Whiting Bay is a mixture of sand, gravel and larger boulders. There are frequently swans, ducks and other interesting waterbirds along the shore and it's a good place for the children to explore. You get great views of Holy Island with the lighthouse buildings, sheer ridges and the mountainous peaks being particularly photogenic when the sun hits them. Whiting Bay is also a notorious place for watching sharks and dolphins.

Eating out in Whiting Bay

For evening meals you are somewhat spoilt for choice in Whiting Bay. The small stretch of hotels (mentioned below) often accommodate for diners who are not necessarily staying at their premises. The Burlington, the Argentine and the Trafalgar (no accommodation) have developed a reputation for high quality cuisine throughout the island and their owners supply a good range of food between them. You will need to book at any of these places.

The Cameronia Hotel (tel: 700254) offers more along the lines of bar food in a more 'public bar' atmosphere and is equally popular with locals and visitors. Here, it's not necessary to book.

Another restaurant which benefits from local acclaim is the 'Pantry'. This is located further along in the village and is often very busy - both at lunch and early evening. (tel: 700489).

Overnight in Whiting Bay

As mentioned, the small hotels are lined up as you enter the village from Lamlash. All offer a similar level of service and 'compete' for a great many visitors who wish to stay here. Contact telephone numbers: Argentine (700662 - owners speak German as well as English), Burlington (700255), Invermay (700431).

There are other smaller hotels and also a surprising number of guest houses in the village including Swans Guest House (tel:700729) and View Bank House (tel:700326).

Naturally, there are yet more Bed and Breakfast homes, self catering units and two camping sites (Cooper Angus Park - tel: 700381 and Burnside Caravan Park which is right at the south end of the village and offers self-catering static caravans - tel: 700381).

You'd be right in assuming that even on the busiest of weekends, you'd rarely find yourself sleeping in the car in Whiting Bay!

CORRIE & SANNOX

Four miles north of Brodick on the eastern coast section of the A841 lay the small villages of Corrie and Sannox. Although distinctly separated by a mile or so, the more northern village of Sannox is so small that Corrie appears to have taken over it's only noticeable man-made facility - the golf course - in name, if nothing else.

Corrie is a pleasant, picturesque village, with red sandstone on the beaches and many remarkably well-maintained homes and gardens. The road weaves around two old harbours (both very small) and the proximity of some of the older homes is so close to the shore that the road is very narrow in places.

Within the village a well-known Arran craftsman, Marvin Elliott, has been able to refurbish and extend the facilities of the local shop and now, along with newspapers and other daily necessities, you can browse around some of Marvin's wood sculptures on display. Next door to the village shop are two craft/gift stores. 'Three Dimensions' (a small but interesting shop which makes unusual clocks and also sells high quality craft goods) and 'Corrie Crafts and Antiques' which has a wide selection of local and imported items. You can park well off the road here or call into Corrie Hotel, with it's popular beer garden on the shore side of the road.

At the more northerly harbour on the bend in the road, visitors will note a large cave entrance. This is the location of the old limestone caves in the village and, unfortunately, little has been done to warn people of the dangers in the area. The caves have been left open and with the effects of rain and large tree roots, they have become so unstable that they are simply too dangerous to explore.

Corrie has the only other real access point to Goatfell (for the main access trail, see the Brodick section). This is located at the southern end of the village (a typical green footpath sign points the way). It's not as popular a route with holiday-makers as it is renowned to be steeper and therefore more tiring. Even if you do only make it halfway up, the views are perhaps not as interesting as those from the Brodick route, but for those people with some hiking experience in this type of terrain, there is the possibility, of course, to use both trails in one day and cover a substantial amount of the eastern portion of the Arran mountains.

Sannox

Sannox is arguably less photogenic than Corrie, but does have two major attractions; a wide crescent-shaped sandy beach and one of Arran's most popular walks up the well-trodden route of Glen Sannox. There are only a few houses that skirt alongside the road, with a smaller hotel, the Ingledene, at the northern end. You can park in one of the lay-bys off to the right for tracks leading to both Glen Sannox and a pleasant little path to the beach, over some stepping stones across the stream.

The Glen Sannox trail is relatively flat, the gradient becoming more steep as you get closer to the base of the mountains and the "Devil's punchbowl" on the left. Walkers, especially those with children and/or dogs should note that there used to be baryte mining in the area and there are still some poorly covered holes in the ground which are not at all safe, so it's best to stick to the path. Also worthy of note is the fact the most people find they have to return on the same route, the sheer mountainsides almost inaccessible for the average walker, except if you plan on venturing over the "saddle" to link up with Glen Rosa and Brodick. This would be a substantial walk, however.

The strangely positioned lights in the hillside here are actually mile-markers for ships and submarines - hopefully 'ours' - many of which operate in the Clyde area.

In Sannox you will also find the Corrie Golf Club. This is one of Arran's less expensive but very enjoyable courses; just nine holes but with very scenic views. A small café within the Golf Course Clubhouse serves teas, coffees and light snacks and is open to non-golfers as well as those who need revitalising after their game. As with most of the smaller courses on Arran, you will find that booking a time is unnecessary, but if you are travelling from a few miles away, always phone to check that there is no competition playing.

Wildlife in the area includes a healthy population of Red Squirrels and there have been numerous sightings of otters. The burn running down from the mountains used to have a fair number of mink, but sightings of these have been rare here recently, although mink do still live on Arran in other areas.

Eating Out in Corrie & Sannox

The Corrie Hotel and the Ingledene Hotel are the only establishments to offer non-residents a lunch or dinner. As mentioned, the tearoom at the golf club is fine for snacks and the Pirate's Cove towards Brodick (see Brodick section) is another choice for dining out.

Overnight in Corrie and Sannox

For anything other than self-catering, you are limited to a few bed and breakfast operations or a choice of three hotels. The red sandstone Corrie Hotel (tel 810273) is the largest and has more services than the smaller but more attractive Blackrock Guest House (tel 810282). In Sannox you have the Ingledene Hotel (tel: 810225), which also serves good food in the evenings and has a garden overlooking the beach.

There are no established campsites in the area.

North Sannox

Visitors seldom notice the village of North Sannox for one main reason - it's no longer there! But, on historical grounds, it is worthy of a mention, even if it strays from the modern-day informative purpose of this book. This area of land, beyond the farmhouse and Pony Trekking facilities offered by Sine McKinnon (tel: 810222) was well populated until the Clearances took effect in the earlier half of the 19th Century. Now, the croft buildings are reduced to low-lying areas of stone and you can just make out the shapes of cottages, fields and walls that are disappearing amongst the bracken.

There is a fairly good walk along the shore here, the car park for which is down the farmhouse track. Locally known as the "Fallen Rocks" path, this route takes you along the shore and, in most cases, will terminate at some significant, you-guessed-it, fallen rocks. You can, of course, opt to carry on beyond the rocks and around the 'Cock of Arran' to Lochranza but bear in mind that this is not only a tough trail in places, it is also one of the most remote areas on the island and not the place to be stuck with a twisted ankle, so take a mobile phone. If you want to see the remoteness of this part of Arran, you are probably better off with the "Laggan" trail in the Lochranza section, which gives you more route options.

"There are many different species of birds of prey in this area of Arran, including Eagles, Owls, Buzzards, Merlins, Hen Harriers, occasional Peregrines and Kestrels"

THE CLEARANCES

Many visitors to Arran wonder about the old ruined croft houses and stone walls which appear all over the island, but particularly on the hillsides at North Sannox. These dwellings were evacuated due to "The Clearances" - perhaps the most significantly bad thing to happen to rural Scotland in the 1800's. Arran didn't escape this economic decision by the land-owners and the following is a brief summary of the effects that led to the Clearances on the island.

In 1766 the trustees of the 7th Duke of Hamilton's estates, asked agriculturalists John Burrel and Boyd Anderson to look into ways of making the Duke's island estate of Arran more profitable. Burrel came over to Arran, carried out several surveys and started a slate quarry as well as searching for coal. He contacted the Duke, suggesting that lime quarries were also opened and that the farm tenants should be allowed to improve their land by removing lime at their own expense.

Burrel also suggested that farms were amalgamated into larger units and that tenant farmers were made directly responsible for the rents and the management of the land. This put pressure on the farmers and the land was therefore only leased to men who could stock, work and improve their area. Of the 1110 families which were supported on the island prior to Burrel's 'improvements', there were to be only 250 which could remain - thereby denying land to over 750 families.

A 'respite' in the form of war against the French enabled most farming communities to hang on until peace came in 1815. The Duke saw opportunities to improve his economic position by sheep grazing. A minister, Headrick, brought sheep to Arran and moved most of them to the north, because of the lack of suitable arable land in the area.

The residents in the area at the time were made homeless by this decision and the Duke paid half the fare of their passage to Canada. In April 1829 a ship left Lamlash with eighty six emigrants for Quebec and further sailings followed. Many Arran people settled in Chaleur Bay; others in Megantic County (still un-touched forest at that time). By 1843 over 220 people from Arran had made new homes in Megantic County alone, either by the Duke's request, or from encouragement by friends who had written from Canada.

Canadian ancestors from the original migrants often visit Arran today.

LOCHRANZA & CATACOL

Almost seven miles of steep roads traverse over the top of the hills from Sannox to Lochranza. 'The Boguillie' road was the last part of the A841 to be built, believe it or not. It is not actually that bad, but if you're a cycling and you've not been using that bike very much in the last few years, beware of the walk ahead! True, the sloping downhill is great as long as you remember the hairpin bends at the bottom of each side of the hill. This is, however, Golden Eagle and Red Deer country. Take a pair of binoculars, walk the newly gravelled path to the base of the mountains (the car park is at the burn, halfway between Lochranza and Sannox) and enjoy the views.

Entering the village of Lochranza you will undoubtedly meet flocks of particularly stupid sheep who have accustomed themselves to divine-wind theories on life and will virtually throw themselves at your vehicle at any opportunity. This has nothing whatsoever to do with the village's appeal - it is one of the more picturesque of Arran's small villages situated, as it is, around a bay with houses on both the north and south sides.

Lochranza is now more commonly known for whisky making as much as anything else. The relatively new Isle of Arran Distillery (tel: 830264) sits just inside the eastern boundary of the village and combines an interesting structural design, guided tours, whisky tasting and a licensed restaurant serving meals and snacks throughout the season. If you're not a whisky drinker it is still a worthwhile facility to see and is another 'key' place to visit on the island. A walk through the whisky-oriented gift shop ends the usual tour of the manufacture of the Arran malt, which has now reached its five-year-old status.

Lying opposite the distillery, Lochranza Golf Club (tel; 830273) extends right up to the shingle beach at the head of the bay. Somewhat dubiously advertised as "the Augusta of Arran" it seems to lack the expected banks of Azaleas and you're more likely to find red deer grazing around the greens. A round of golf is relatively inexpensive and there are pleasant areas of streams and mature trees throughout the course. Here, too, is the campsite that can get very busy in peak season. Services are well organised for those staying for several nights or more and it's less than half a mile from the hotel, shop and other services in the village.

Lochranza's village shop supplies the usual range of necessities, newspapers and postal services for the village. Open all year round, with extended hours in the summer, this is also the place to ask for the key to unlock the castle which stands on the prominent spur of land in the bay.

The castle ruins, estimated to be around 850 years old comprise a small but interesting structure having been re-built by various former inhabitants. There are wall plaques and an information board which explain the history of the site. In the summer it is not uncommon to see scaffolding against the castle walls. This is a rendering contract lasting an unfortunate ten years but at least it will maintain the structure as it is for some time to come.

A small butcher's shop lies at the last corner of the road towards the main pier and a very busy tearoom serves coffees, teas, snacks and meals every day, especially handy if you are waiting to catch the ferry to Claonaig, on the mainland.

Visitors who arrive in Lochranza by boat will find six blue buoys that are free to use. Lochranza, however, is popular with yachting enthusiasts from Loch Fyne, Tarbert and Campbeltown, so arrive early unless you are happy anchoring on the northern side of the bay, where it's deeper and safer. A small slipway about 100 yards east of the main ferry slipway is the preferred place to come ashore on a dinghy.

The local hall (newly built at the incredible cost of nearly half a million pounds), lies next to the village green and hosts many musical evenings of various types throughout the summer. You can normally find out what is "going on" at the shop, or at either of the two hotels.

There are a number of local craft shops in the village, two of which are decidedly off the beaten track. The Lochranza Studio gallery is located past the surgery and lies alongside the golf course on the track leading to 'Laggan'. You can't really drive up here and parking is best found further back in the village, but the walk to the gallery is short and scenic and there is artwork for sale, painted by the resident owners. By far the most unusually located craftshop on Arran, The Whins, sits halfway up the hill above the Newton (north) shore. There are two tracks leading to the shop (one is a gravel track just off the road, the other a grassy sheep-path well along the shore) neither of which are too strenuous. The shop owner makes 'Arran Stonemen' amongst other unique products. The view from here is superb and there are many places to picnic close by.

The curiously named 'Green Harper Gallery' is located at the impressive 'Castlekirk' house close to the castle and sells one-off sculptures and paintings by local and visiting artists.

As mentioned, there is a small health centre in Lochranza, open at specific hours of the week. Opening hours are posted on the building, which lies opposite the Field Centre.

The numerous white buildings of Lochranza Field Centre cater for groups who are studying the noteable geological interest of the area as well as the geography of Arran. This explains the groups of brightly clad students massed in small groups along the beaches or knee deep in the streams with surveying equipment!

A good but often overlooked walk to Laggan starts at the junction between the Newton shore road and the spur road past the surgery. This is a long walk, and it gets boggy right on the top of the hill. However, if you follow the signs to Laggan (an old settlement long vacated) you will find the track very clear and once you are on the top of the hill you will have great views of the northern part of the Clyde estuary and Bute. You can return the same way, or walk the grassy but steep path down to the shore. From here turning right along the coast will take you on a long trek to Sannox; turning left will take you past some ruined crofts, wide areas of sandstone beach and some interesting rockpools. This trail, to Lochranza, disappears in heavy fallen rocks and you will need to exercise a lot of care scrambling through them until the beach reappears about 100 yards on. At the end of the track, just as you begin to see the houses of Lochranza, a small stone circle is visible on the side of the beach. There is no history to this, other than the fact that it is less than five years old and was built by a local - celebrating his marriage! In these hills, too, is "Fairy Glen". This very secret and not always easily found area is located by walking the higher track around Newton Shore, then down towards the beach. You'll pass by the glen on your descent.

Catacol

A mile and a half south west of Lochranza on the western coast, the small hamlet of Catacol sits at the base of steep cliffs which give way to a small area of farmland and a Catacol Glen which leads to Loch Tanna. This small cluster of houses includes one of Arran's most famous architectural sights - the 'twelve apostles' - a row of terraced houses with the curious quirk of each having a different shaped upper window frame. The services in Catacol are limited to the local public house, the Catacol Bay Hotel.

At the bridge in Catacol there is a relatively large car park for the much-walked route to Loch Tanna. The trail is good, but it's long. Weather here can change rapidly due to the high hills around and many people, especially those with children, never make it as far as the loch (Arran's largest) because of a change in weather, or the rather un-scenic views (you quickly lose sight of the sea). However, it is an interesting walk, following the stream all the way, with always the possibility to see an otter. There are also several large boulders mid-stream that make excellent picnic tables!

Eating out in Lochranza & Catacol

The Lochranza Distillery (tel: 830264) offers the most upmarket food in the area, often busy during the day and bookings are advised during the evenings. It's pleasant, but if it's too quiet the atmosphere can be a little impersonal. Lochranza Hotel (tel: 830223) offers food every day and the often busy bar (the hotel is close by to the Field Centre and Youth Hostel) bar can be smoky. The Pier Tearoom (tel: 830217) caters for busy ferry traffic and supplies travellers with morning coffees, afternoon teas and snacks. At the time of going to press, the tearoom is changing ownership, so call ahead for the latest details on food availability.
Catacol Bay Hotel (tel: 830231) serves popular bar meals in an often busy and friendly environment. The pub is well known locally for live entertainment year-round at the hotel, and as event hosts at the village hall.

A carry-out service is possible for food and drink which is handy if you're camping or self catering in the area.

Overnight in Lochranza & Catacol

A few well sign-posted bed and breakfast homes still operate in both villages although self catering units are now quite rare and often booked up by regular visitors. Camping is available at the Lochranza Golf complex and there are comprehensive facilities here. The Youth Hostel (tel: 830631) caters for travellers both young and old. You are required to return to the hostel by a certain hour each evening before the front doors are locked. Lochranza Hotel (tel: 830223) and Catacol Bay Hotel (tel: 830231) both offer functional and fairly typical "inn accommodation" to travellers. The Catacol Bay Hotel also has a self-catering unit in the village.

ARRAN'S RED DEER

The red deer on Arran are reported to be among the largest animals of their kind in Scotland, possibly thanks to the mild winters. However, there has been a very sporadic rate of growth in their population over the past few years and declines in numbers are due to poor quality grazing in the mountains (hence the fact that they like to visit local gardens!). There have also been man-made disasters affecting their normal habitat. In May 2001 a couple of hikers left a portable barbecue burning (so the story goes) in the Glen Rosa valley. Five days later when the fire was finally put out, there was a 'patch' of burnt ground almost a mile across which spread from Glen Rosa to Dougarie on the west coast (almost 10 miles). It is also common practice for routine culling of older stags to take place. This is 'deer management' but it's also a source of income for landowners who take those who can afford it on a day's shoot. A hill-phone service operates to let walkers know if they are likely to be in any area where shooting takes place (tel: 302363).
Regardless of this, there are plenty of deer on the hills - and in the villages in the north of the island. You rarely need binoculars to see them and, in spring, there's always the chance of finding an antler to grace your front door. (just make sure that the one you want isn't still attached to the animal!).

SHISKINE & BLACKWATERFOOT

Once you have negotiated the String Road's bends and hills, the valley at Shiskine opens out considerably and, at once, you realise just how substantially different this area of the island is compared to the north or east. A small spur road, leading over Machrie Moor to Machrie and Dougarie is a handy short cut to take to the west coast. (note the unusual post box at the junction). Continuing on the String Road, however, will lead you through the fields of the Shiskine Valley.

Balmichael Visitor Centre

Just before you reach the village a visitor centre at Balmichael is one of Arran's larger attractions and there are some very interesting shops and craft businesses here, as well as a café and outdoor activities for both children and adults in the form of quad biking. An adventure playground and a putting green are also popular.

The very picturesque courtyard at Balmichael Visitor Centre (pronounced Bal-Mickel) is a very well kept and a pleasant place to wander around the various shops. Simon Thorborn, of Arran Ceramics, has his pottery here and has many pieces on display and for sale. Particularly interesting are the Raku vases and lamp-stands. There is also an antique shop, with a wide selection of relatively small (and therefore easy to carry) antiques with a few modern gift ideas. Moorland Crafts, who also have a jewellery shop ("Island Treasure") at the centre, sell a wide range of mostly inexpensive gifts including a host of ideas for children to spend their holiday money on. There is a comprehensively stocked shop, Trareoch Crafts, which specialises in d.i.y craft supplies, particularly needlework and tapestries, amongst other gift selections.
The café, in the old mill building, can be busy but there are several tables outside if the weather is fine enough.

The village of Shiskine, the only village to be situated away from the coast, holds little of interest for the visitor - there are no shops or visitor attractions and the area seems to many as the residential part of Blackwaterfoot, albeit a couple of miles away. There is, however, the Arran Outdoor Centre located in Shiskine. The centre is used for pre-booked group activities and The Abernethy Trust minibuses which can be seen around the island are those belonging to the facility.

There is also a surgery in Shiskine, at Inglewood (a large house, but tucked away off the road) and open hours are displayed on the surgery wall). The surgery is located just past the Old House Boarding Cattery, where you can book in your cat for it's own holiday. (tel: 860302)

A small spur road at the junction in the village (just beside one of the only bed and breakfast homes in Shiskine, at Roadend, tel: 860448), is a quick route through to Torbeg and links to the A841 north of Blackwaterfoot. This short, straight spur road has a particularly evil bump right in the middle of it!

Back in Shiskine and heading south to the village of Blackwaterfoot, the String Road that you have been on for some 8 miles or so soon ends at the junction of the A841, just east of the village. You can turn right into the village itself, or left, taking you through the small hamlet of Kilpatrick. In Kilpatrick you will find Port-na-Lochan Fishery, a small but very well constructed man-made trout fishery which is open to the general public throughout the year. The owner, George Bannatyne, lives next door in Lochside Guest House (see later) and runs the fishery for individuals and groups, with both fly fishing and bait fishing available. You can hire tackle and buy trout without necessarily having to fish for them. There is, of course, a daily limit on the number of fish you can take home and prices for fishing the small loch are very reasonable. (tel: 860276).

If you continue on the road south past Kilpatrick, the shore becomes very distant as you ascend the cliffs and follow the signs to, eventually, Kilmory, Kildonan and Whiting Bay. These areas are covered in their own sections.

Back at the Shiskine junction you turn right into Blackwaterfoot. One of the most popular outdoor activities on the island, pony trekking, can be done here, courtesy of Cairnhouse Riding Centre. In fact, it's a little more than pony trekking as owner Dawn Murchie also runs riding classes as well as more 'adventurous' two-hour hacks in the afternoon with more experienced riders. Riders of any age and experience are welcomed and there are pleasant treks through the village and along the beach if the tide is out. (tel: 860466).

A & C Cameron (tel: 860277) run a busy garage and repair centre at Blackwaterfoot (petrol is also available here) as well as one of the two village shops, next door. This is also the village post office (tel: 860220). A small bakery tucked down the small side street before you reach the Kinloch Hotel, is also here. However, it's the Kinloch Hotel itself which is very much the centre of the village, mainly because of its surprising size in such an area of low population. The hotel, one of the largest on the island, is an interesting, light grey structure, with some almost continental architectural designs. There have been a number of extensions and improvements to the hotel, both inside and out and yet there still remains the feel of a typical beach resort hotel that you would expect to find on the south coast of England. Large lounges, with huge windows, overlook the sea to the west. The hotel is now under the "Best Western" brand, but is still run by the Crawford family, in residence now for many years. A swimming pool is popular with residents and there are other bar games such as pool and darts.

The central part of the village is also noticeable for it's attractive bridge over the stream which rushes into the sea. It's a nice area to sit, although you're never far from the road or the large car park, and there are some benches and grassy areas for picnics. If you want to get away from the road, take a short walk down the car park, following the beach along a small track in front of the houses. You can walk for miles along here and there are some small sections of sandy beach (though not as prominent as the main beach of Blackwaterfoot at the Golf Club end of the village).

One of Arran's main butchers, Donald Galbraith, operates his shop from Blackwaterfoot, just north of the bridge. The extensive range of meats, pies and so on is well-known throughout the island and you'll see Donald's products in village shops all around Arran.

Opposite the butchers is Blackwaterfoot's other village shop, The Harbour Shop (tel: 860215). It's a typical village store, with that little-bit-of-everything in a small unit. Such is the nature of many shops on Arran in small communities which have to buy for the tourist as much as maintain the demand for specific goods for the locals.

Turning along a short section of road (to keep close to the shore) just beyond the new houses, the Shiskine Golf and Tennis Club is located. It's a very popular area, not least because of the potential to keep the entire family happy in one go, thanks to the sporting facilities and the wide expanse of (mostly) sandy beach. The Golf Club (tel: 860226) has a small but functional clubhouse and you can usually turn up for a round of golf whenever you like, although, like almost all courses on Arran, it's advisable to phone ahead to check that there are no competitions or events taking place. On busier days, especially weekends, you may need to call for a tee-off time. Obviously not entirely happy with the fact that useable land in the area is extremely valuable, the course is unusual in that it has 12 holes. This makes for an interesting game and there are a few very tricky holes to master. The nature of the course has been well documented and has appeared on television more than once. Invariably, this has helped maintain a good number of visitors, as well as local members, and the facility is very well presented.

On the road heading north, up the west coast, there's little until you reach Torbeg. Here you'll dicover, just tucked off the main road on that spur road from Shiskine I mentioned earlier, the Glendale Gallery. The gallery is run by Jim and Eunice Williamson who show a range of paintings (many by Jim) and other arts and crafts from the area. It's a small, friendly and interesting gallery so don't forget it on your whizz past to the Kings Cave car park.

KINGS CAVE

About 4 miles from Blackwaterfoot a large (ish) Forestry Commission car park advertises the Kings Cave walk. There is an information board here, detailing the path, which is very obvious once you're on it - this is an extremely popular walk and therefore well trodden. The trail follows the edge of the forest, with some great views of Machrie and the western coast as far as Dougarie. On warm, still days remember to take some insect repellent - the trees you walk alongside attract bugs of every kind. The trail is surprisingly longer than most people think and children often get a little despondent. A reminder of the cave ahead always seems to do the trick. Once you reach a small canyon in the rock, you're nearly on the beach and the you simply follow the shoreline to the cave. The cave itself is a giant hollow rather than a maze of tunnels, but it's interesting to ponder whether this was, indeed, where Robert the Bruce saw the spider. Your designated driver could return for the car and meet you back in Blackwaterfoot (at the golf club) but it's more likely that you will choose to return the same way as it's a slightly easier walk.

Note that although you can see almost all there is to see at the cave, entrance to the cave may be difficult due to the fact that railings have been installed outside the cave entrance. Keys are normally only given to outdoor education parties, but you never know - there may be a group there when you visit.

The tourist board have details of weekly guided tours of Kings Cave.

Eating out in the Shiskine & Blackwaterfoot

Shiskine, being almost entirely residential, offers no food services of any kind, except for the day-time tearoom at Balmichael Visitor Centre. Blackwaterfoot's Kinloch Hotel (tel: 860444) and the cosier Blackwaterfoot Lodge (the former Blackwaterfoot Hotel - now under new management- tel: 860202) both serve meals throughout the day.

Accommodation in Shiskine & Blackwaterfoot.

Several private self-catering units operate in the village and the aforementioned hotels supply well-serviced overnight accommodation. The Kinloch has a pool.

THE WEST COAST

The road north of Blackwaterfoot and up the west coast of Arran is much quieter than the eastern side of the island, mainly because of the lack of any significant developments in the area - business or residential. It's therefore a more tranquil drive than the other areas of Arran and you will often find long stretches of road with no other traffic. Although the villages are more spread out (and much smaller), there are more houses visibly standing in their own grounds or part of the estate lands which throughout run the north-west area of the island. The area has not been artificially forested and therefore many older homes and farmsteads have been renovated or have simply maintained occupation since long ago. The west coast is a great place to sit in the evening sun - a privilege which you may not always enjoy in areas of the eastern side of Arran due to the mountains obstructing the horizon. Arran has some glorious sunsets, helped by the clarity of the air and the occasional intermittent cloud cover which adds to the attraction.

The road, then, takes you north from Blackwaterfoot, passing Torbeg and the start of the very spread out homes of Machrie. The road is narrow and very twisty in places - remember those oncoming buses!

"Tennis courts at Machrie are in close proximity to the first fairway of the golf course!"

Machrie Moor Standing Stones

The standing stones of Machrie Moor are well-known throughout Scotland. What they actually represented is still a mystery but theories on Astronomy, Rituals and other more bizarre suggestions are often read and heard about.
Although the stones themselves are miniscule compared to those at Stonehenge, for example, the walk is flat, not too long and in the evening especially there is the possibility of photographing an Arran sunset with the obelisks in the foreground, giving a very evocative picture.
A small carpark (really *too* small - and the road is unfortunately much too narrow to park on) is located on the opposite side of the road to the path that starts you on your walk. It's a mile or so to the stones, the terrain is occasionally muddy but the majority of the route is stony and dry, especially at the start of the walk. It's not unusual for the trail to be busy and visitors, especially children running around the stones, often get in the way of that elusive 'National Geographic style' photo you were hoping to achieve!

The land remains cultivated in sections until you reach the Machrie Golf Course area, where the spur road that connects with the String road to Brodick cuts across the bracken and heather of Machrie Moor.

The golf course is one of the most popular 9-hole courses and is by far the most laid back in it's approach. You simply turn up and pay for a round (there's an honesty box if the clubhouse/tearoom is closed). Because of it's appeal to holidaymakers and locals who want to have an inexpensive but enjoyable round, it does get busy - especially in late afternoon/evening when the sun is still high in the western sky. The course is well-maintained and with the lack of trees or water hazards most holes are uneventful if you hit the ball straight! The tearoom is popular with golfers and non-golfers although outdoor seating is not provided, due to the close proximity of the road and the first fairway!

The beaches on the west coast are mostly of rock and shingle, with good patches of sand at low tides. There are numerous birds to look out for along the coastline, particularly gannets, cormorants, guillemots, and fulmars. In the north, towards Lochranza, you'll also find grebes, divers and mergansers. This is also the start of the red deer habitat and the sporting estate at Dougarie holds the shooting rights here, as well as salmon fishing in the river Iorsa (contact Dougarie Lodge on 840259).

Just south of Dougarie Lodge, a signpost to the 'Old Byre Showroom' is worth further investigation. You drive up the old farm track (notice the standing stones in the field as well as game birds near the roadside) and park in the old farmyard. The Old Byre has a shop in Brodick, but this is their headquarters and a diverse range of sheepskin, leather and woollen goods are sold here. (tel: 840227)

After the bends in the road at Dougarie, you are often tempted to pull up onto the shoulder and walk along the beach. There are some fine rockpools along this stretch, some good chances of picking up a piece of driftwood or seashells and great places to picnic on the shore side. Just before the road starts to climb towards Whitefarland, a small parking area (un-signposted, but fairly obvious) indicates another walk you can try under the cliffs. This takes you along a grassy trail and then lands you on the stony beach under the tall cliffs which are often full of nesting gulls. This is a great area for taking your dog as you're away from the busier beaches and there is rarely anyone else around to worry about.

The road climbs dramatically up to Whitefarland where a large farm at the top is located at a bend in the road. There is a fair chance of having to brake quickly for hens, ducks and other, seemingly suicidal, birds on the road. You haven't left the shore for very long and once you've descended you are welcomes by several of Arran's palm trees, next to the attractive houses of Whitefarland. This is a tiny hamlet, with no services and people rarely stop until they reach Pirnmill, a couple of miles up the road.

Pirnmill

With historic herring fishing roots, the village of Pirnmill hangs on to a small population, but nevertheless has enough by way of services to keep many visitors from simply driving through. A small post office and general store (tel: 850235) sits next-door to the newly named 'Lighthouse Tearoom' (formerly the 'Anvil'). You can get anything here from all-day breakfasts to a full evening dinner and the tearoom is open all season (tel: 850240). At low tide in Pirnmill there is a section of sandy beach (opposite the primary school) which is almost the last significant stretch of sand you will see until you are in Sannox (or Blackwaterfoot if heading south). It's not a big bit of beach, but should keep the kids happy!

Pirnmill quickly disappears as the road starts to look threatening to the north. Between Pirnmill and Catacol you have to drive over some of the most unusual features of this 'A class' road. The geology of the area forced early road builders to simply accept the shape of the land and this means you have a series of small blind summits to cross over. It doesn't last long, but note that doing anything over 15 miles an hour and you will likely add to all those exhaust pipe scrape-marks on the tarmac! Passengers will note, however, that the beach here looks more interesting and there is a large layby just after the 'bumps' where it is worth pulling over and walking back along the beach to explore some of the weirdest sea-line rock structures you'll find on the island.

Back on the road, another couple of bumps takes you round the sweeping bend at Glen Catacol and into the villages of Catacol and Lochranza.

Eating out on the west coast

The 'Lighthouse' and Machrie Bay tearooms, already mentioned, are the only eating establishments between Catacol and Blackwaterfoot.

Overnight on the west coast.
There are a number of small self-catering units in the area (Dougarie Lodge has more, but you'll need to book well in advance). There are no hotels or guest houses between Catacol and Blackwaterfoot.

KILDONAN & KILMORY

The southeast corner of Arran is an area of cliffs, seal colonies and inland forests. There are several small villages both on, and off, the main road. One particular note of interest are the two small islands of Pladda (close to Kildonan and with a lighthouse on it) and Ailsa Craig, a conical-shaped bird sanctuary and somewhat further out on the southern horizon. Both islands are not accessible to most, however, but they do make interesting viewing from the south coast.

The road from Whiting Bay rises well above the shore line and takes you around the southeast corner at Dippen. The high cliffs and often pounding waves make this area very quiet as far as visitor traffic is concerned and you really won't see much until you take the first of two side roads down to the village of Kildonan.

The loop around the village and back to the main road is worth taking, especially if you wish to stop off for lunch or picnic along the beach. Grey seals are very much in evidence along the coastline and there are large sections of sandy beach close to the ruins of Kildonan Castle (so ruined, there's not much to see). You can park here on a large grassy area, close to a standing stone, and walk the short distance to the shore. Just along the road are the few businesses in the area, the Kildonan and Breadalbane Hotels, a small campsite and further on a village shop, Kildonan Stores, which is also the post office (tel: 820275). There are a few signposted walks in and around the village and parking is best for these at the school house area, rather than on the road. You could, if you wished, walk from here along the shore for several miles towads Kilmory.

Back on the main road, Southbank Farm Park (tel: 820221) is a collection of rare farm breeds, sheepdog demonstrations and other farm-related attractions. The farm is an interesting day out and probably unexpected to most people who come to Arran for other reasons. However, it's a good venue to take children and it's not too far a journey from the main villages.

There are several longer walks north of the road near Kildonan, mainly involving treks through forested areas to areas such as Loch Garbad. Many of these trails are not listed in conventional walk books of Arran, but the views from the hills looking south take some beating. There are a lot of small streams and minor waterfalls in the area which add to the scenery but also mean that walking boots of water-tight nature may be required as the pathways can get quite boggy after rainfall.

Back on the road, heading west to Kilmory, there is little to see until you reach this small village. Unusually for such a low populated area on Arran, you will come across one of Arran's older businesses, which has a small visitor centre. Torrylinn Creamery (tel: 870240) is predominantly a cheese-making operation and you can learn about how it is made on a small commercial basis from their informative staff and literature. The Arran Dunlop cheese (similar to a red cheddar) which is made here is well-known around the UK and you can buy it here, or at other shops around the island.

There is a farm track next door to the Creamery which leads to a very large, safe sandy beach. This wide, long stretch of sand, with a shallow drop-off into the sea is perfect for a day on the beach and there are areas of rockpools at either end. Although it's one of Arran's most popular beaches, there's never a large number of people around (partly because it's not visible from the road and therefore often missed). You do, however, have to park somewhere in the village and walk the half mile or so to the shore.

A small craftshop, the Kilmory Workshop is well signposted and the village is also home to Island Porcelain - a well-established craft business that specialises in porcelain seabirds such as puffins and gannets. They are ideal souvenirs and gifts for those who are 'difficult to buy for'.

The local shop and post office in the village is not immediately obvious to those searching for it. In fact, you have to drive a small way west of the main village to the small hamlet of Lagg. This tiny collection of buildings is located in a picturesque little valley and is the last point that you'll be able to stop for shopping or food until you reach Blackwaterfoot, about seven miles further on. There are a few small walks in the area, another sandy beach at "Cleats Shore" and an opportunity to see grey herons in the trees. You can stop off for lunch at the hotel which has some picnic tables outside. Behind the hotel, Alison Bell has a small silk painting gallery and workshop. Alison's work is well-known and she has customers all over the world, so it's worth calling in to see her at Arran Fine Art Silks (tel: 870344).

The village shop, just opposite the hotel carries the usual necessities, groceries and limited postal services. Don't forget, the 'last post' in rural areas such as here leaves as early as 2.30pm.

Once you've driven down into Lagg and up the other side the road still takes you well away from the shoreline as the southwest cliffs of the island take over the area and the road is forced to go over the top of the hills. You will quickly reach the Ross road turning for Lamlash (it's actually more scenic to drive it from this end) and after the junction there are several other rougher tracks, mostly leading to farm houses.

Eating out in Kildonan and Kilmory

Meals and snacks are available from the three hotels in the area, the Kildonan (tel: 820207), the Breadalbane (tel: 820284) and the Lagg Inn (tel: 870255). The Lagg Inn is very much a coaching-inn type of establishment and has a busy bar at the weekends. The others are quieter, catering mainly for residents and people staying at the camp site in Kildonan or at self catering units nearby.

Overnight in Kildonan and Kilmory

The three establishments listed above have letting accommodation. If you want a sea view, remember that the Lagg is located away from the shore, but it's quieter location may appeal to those looking for more tranquil surroundings. The Kildonan and the Breadalbane both offer fairly typical sea-front accommodation and although services are perhaps not as numerous as those in larger villages, the hotels appeal to those looking for a holiday where indoor facilities are not on the top of their agenda.
A campsite ('Seal Shore' tel: 820320) is also located in Kildonan, close to the Kildonan Hotel. It has a toilet block and other limited services for both caravans and tents.

SLIDDERY & CORRIECRAVIE

Between Lagg and Blackwaterfoot you will find yourself on the loneliest piece of the main road and there's really not a great deal to stop for. You can, however, often make out the coast of Northern Ireland on a clear day.

You'll soon be through the small areas of Sliddery and Corriecravie, each having little (if anything) by way of facilities aside from a few remote bed and breakfast or self catering units.

As you round the southwest corner towards Blackwaterfoot, you should also be able to see (easily) the far tip of Kintyre (the famous "Mull") and, further up, Davaar Island near Campbeltown on the Kintyre Peninsula. Navy vessels and fishing trawlers are often seen up and down the Kilbrannan sound between Arran and Kintyre - keep an eye out for submarines, too.

"The majority of cattle farming and dairy herds on Arran are located between Kildonan and Blackwaterfoot. If you want to see Highland Cattle, there are small herds near Kildonan & Kilmory."

VILLAGE MAPS

The following pages show maps of Brodick, Lamlash, Whiting Bay, Lochranza and Blackwaterfoot. Although not to scale, they indicate the locations of various businesses, services and facilities within each village, corresponding to items of text in the main body of the book.

There is a road map of Arran on page 89 which mentions most of the island's visitor centres, golf courses and other areas of interest.

BRODICK

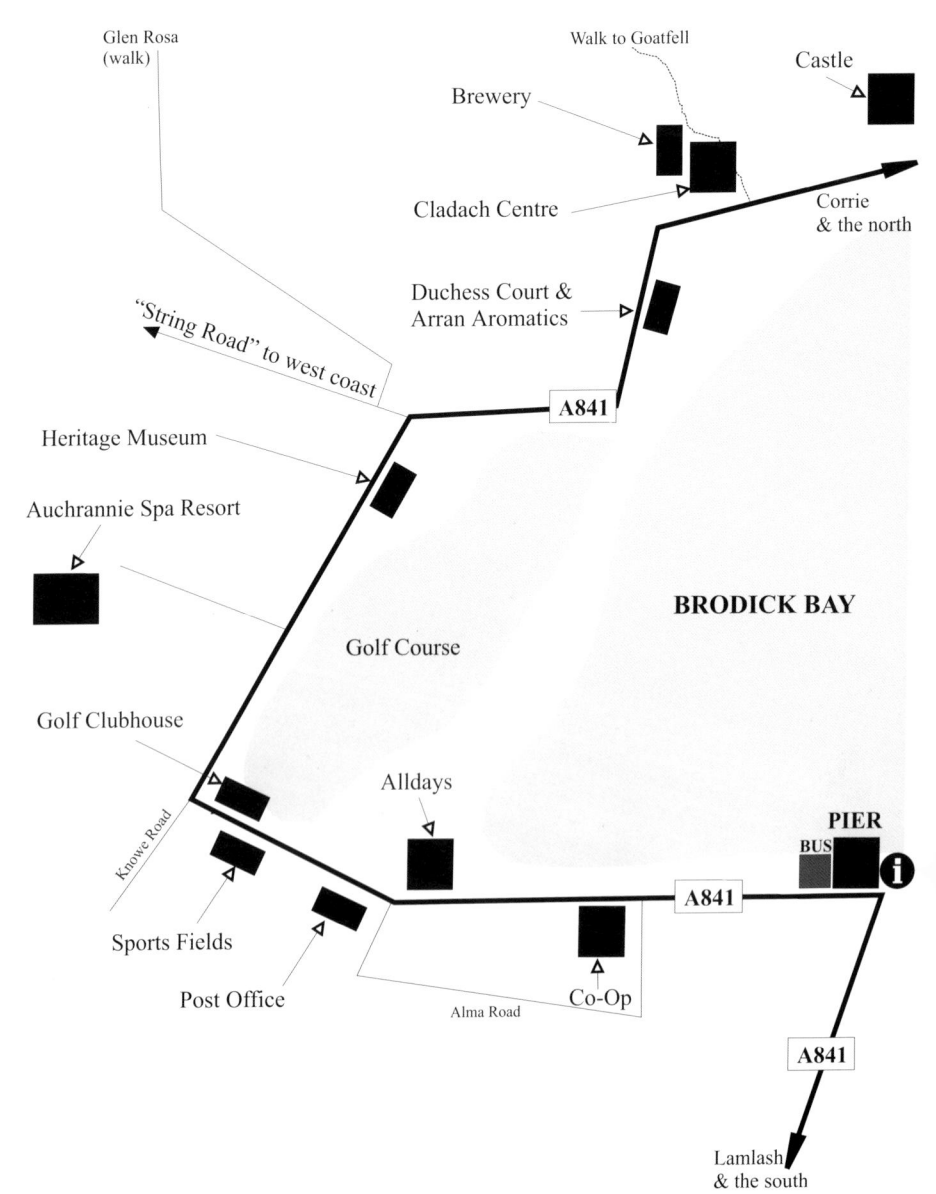

Glen Rosa (walk)

Walk to Goatfell

Castle

Brewery

Cladach Centre

Corrie & the north

Duchess Court & Arran Aromatics

"String Road" to west coast

A841

Heritage Museum

Auchrannie Spa Resort

BRODICK BAY

Golf Course

Golf Clubhouse

Alldays

PIER
BUS

Knowe Road

Sports Fields

Post Office

Alma Road

Co-Op

A841

A841

Lamlash & the south

LAMLASH

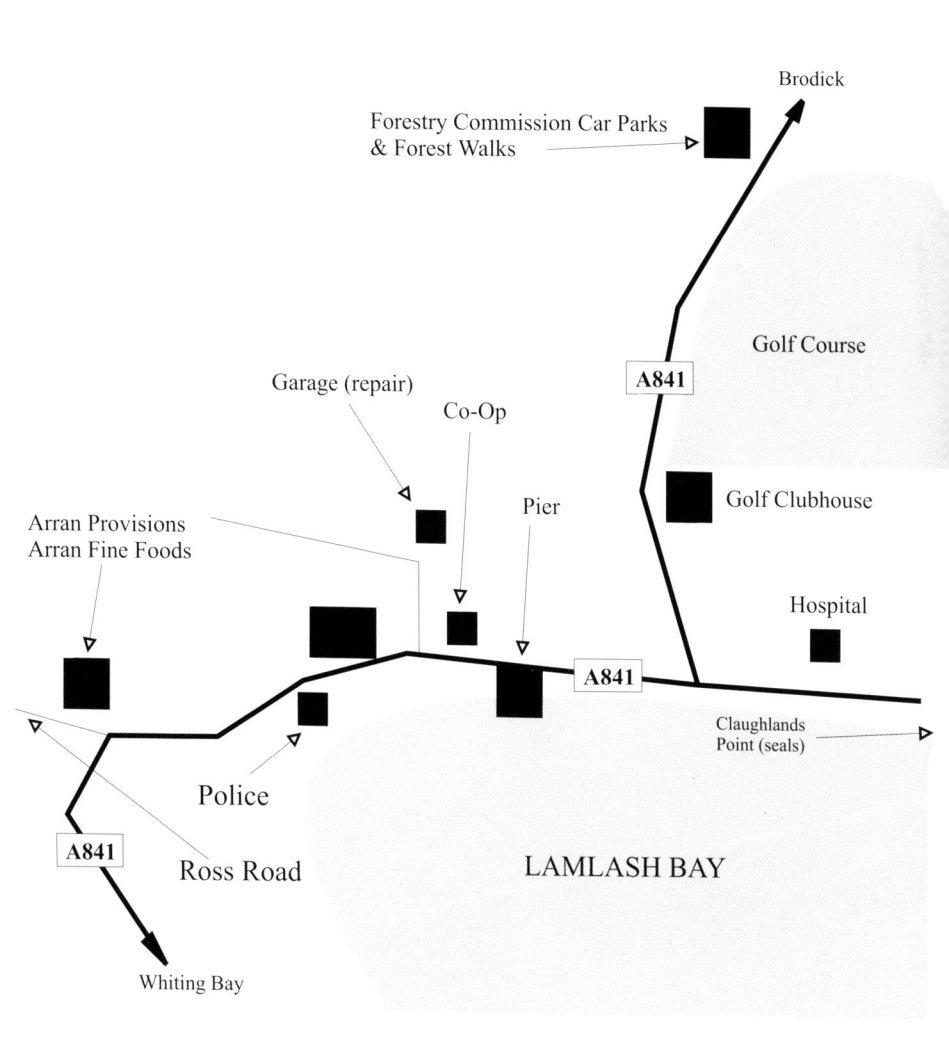

WHITING BAY

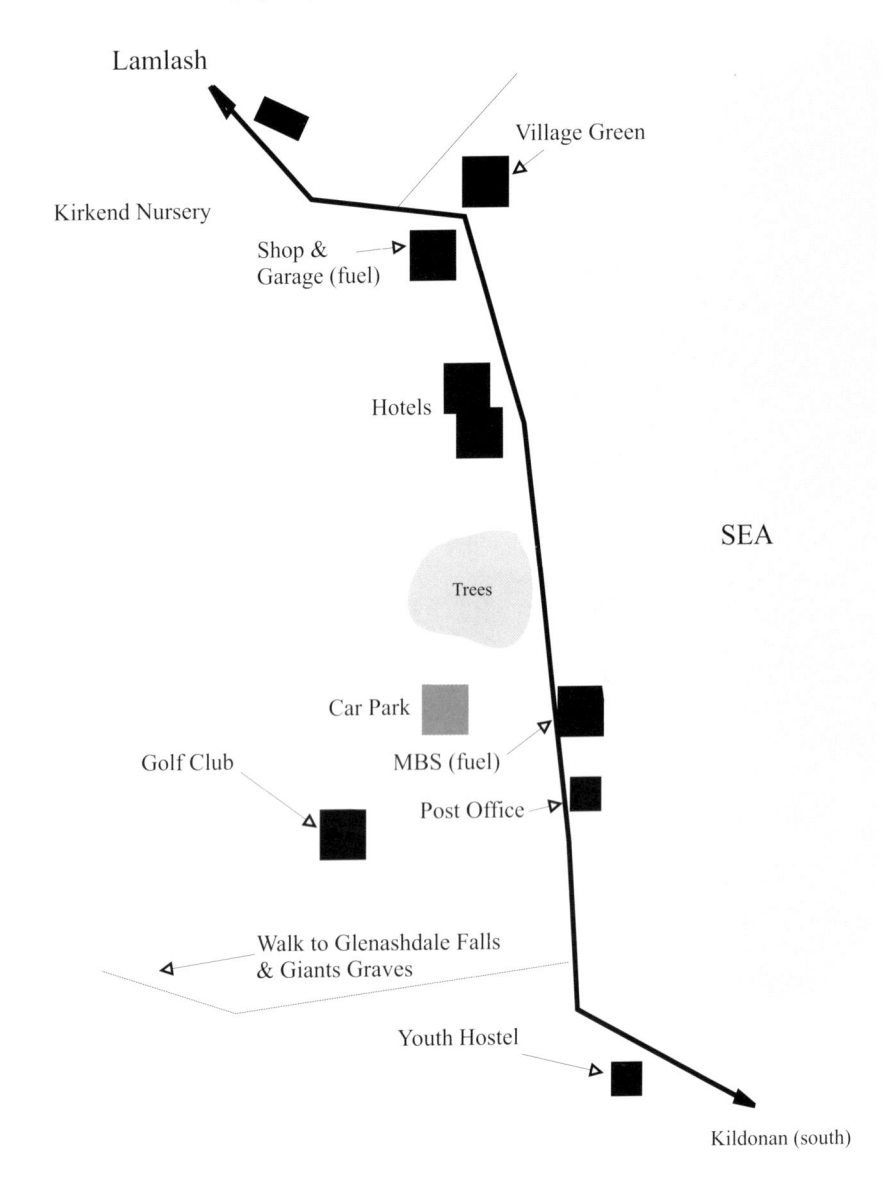

LOCHRANZA

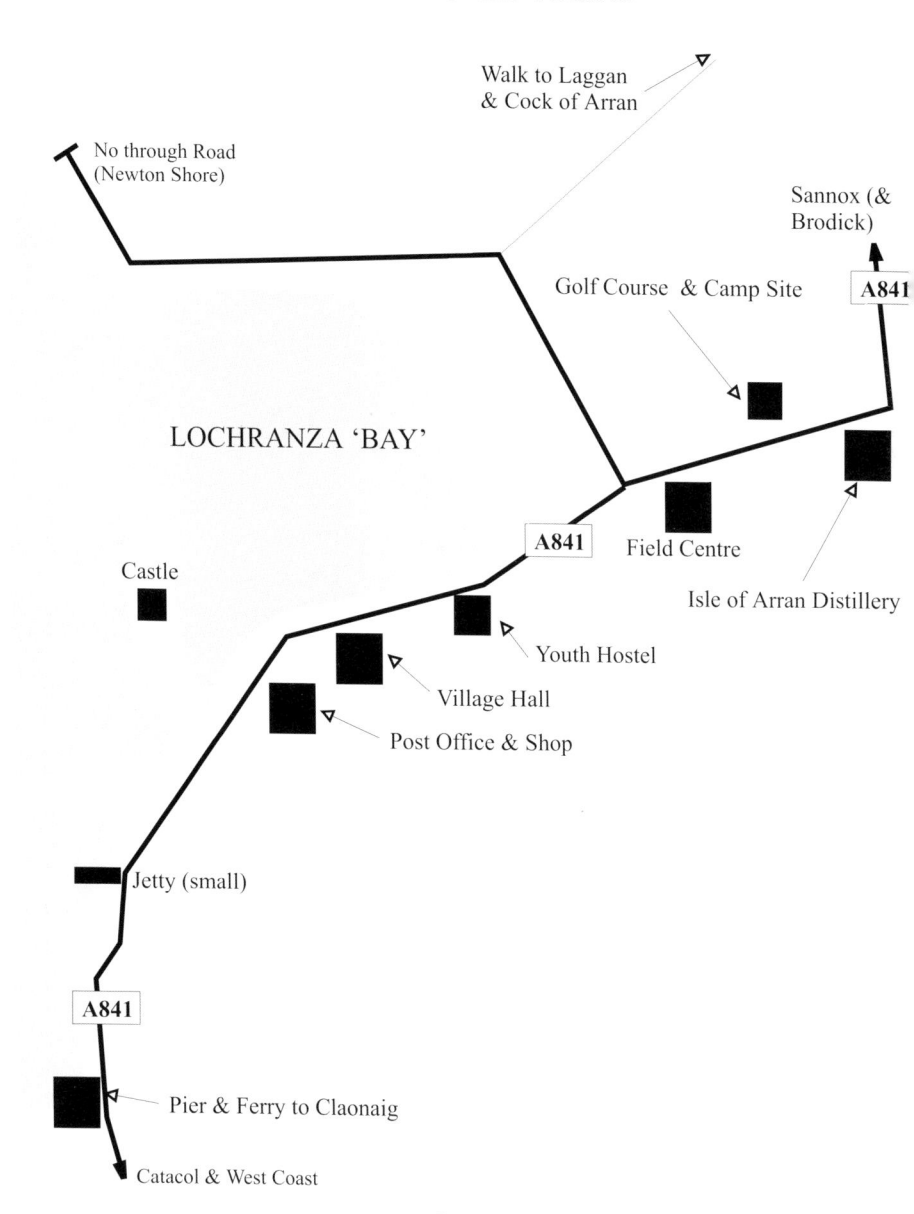

Walk to Laggan & Cock of Arran

No through Road (Newton Shore)

Sannox (& Brodick)

A841

Golf Course & Camp Site

LOCHRANZA 'BAY'

A841

Field Centre

Isle of Arran Distillery

Castle

Youth Hostel

Village Hall

Post Office & Shop

Jetty (small)

A841

Pier & Ferry to Claonaig

Catacol & West Coast

BLACKWATERFOOT

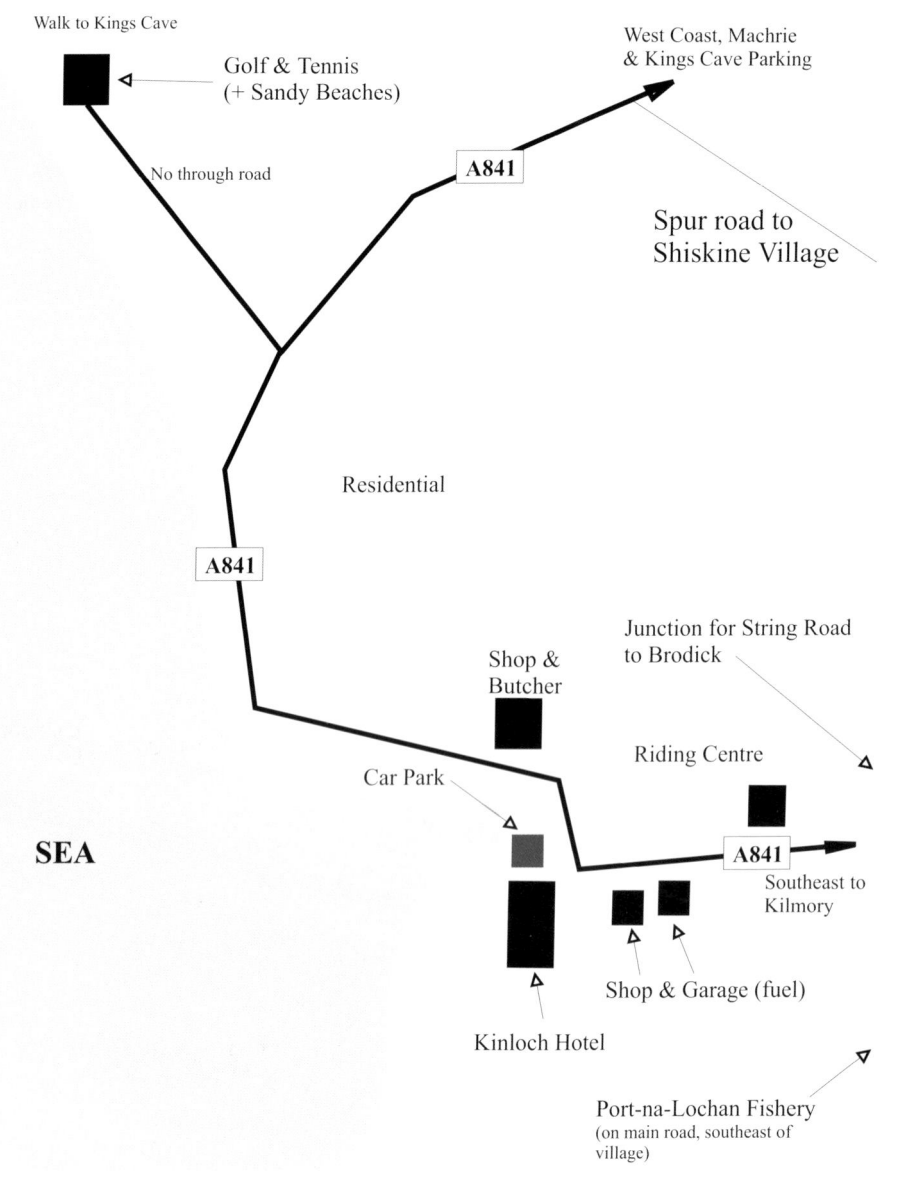

Walk to Kings Cave

Golf & Tennis
(+ Sandy Beaches)

West Coast, Machrie
& Kings Cave Parking

No through road

A841

Spur road to
Shiskine Village

Residential

A841

Junction for String Road
to Brodick

Shop &
Butcher

Riding Centre

Car Park

SEA

A841

Southeast to
Kilmory

Shop & Garage (fuel)

Kinloch Hotel

Port-na-Lochan Fishery
(on main road, southeast of
village)

MAP

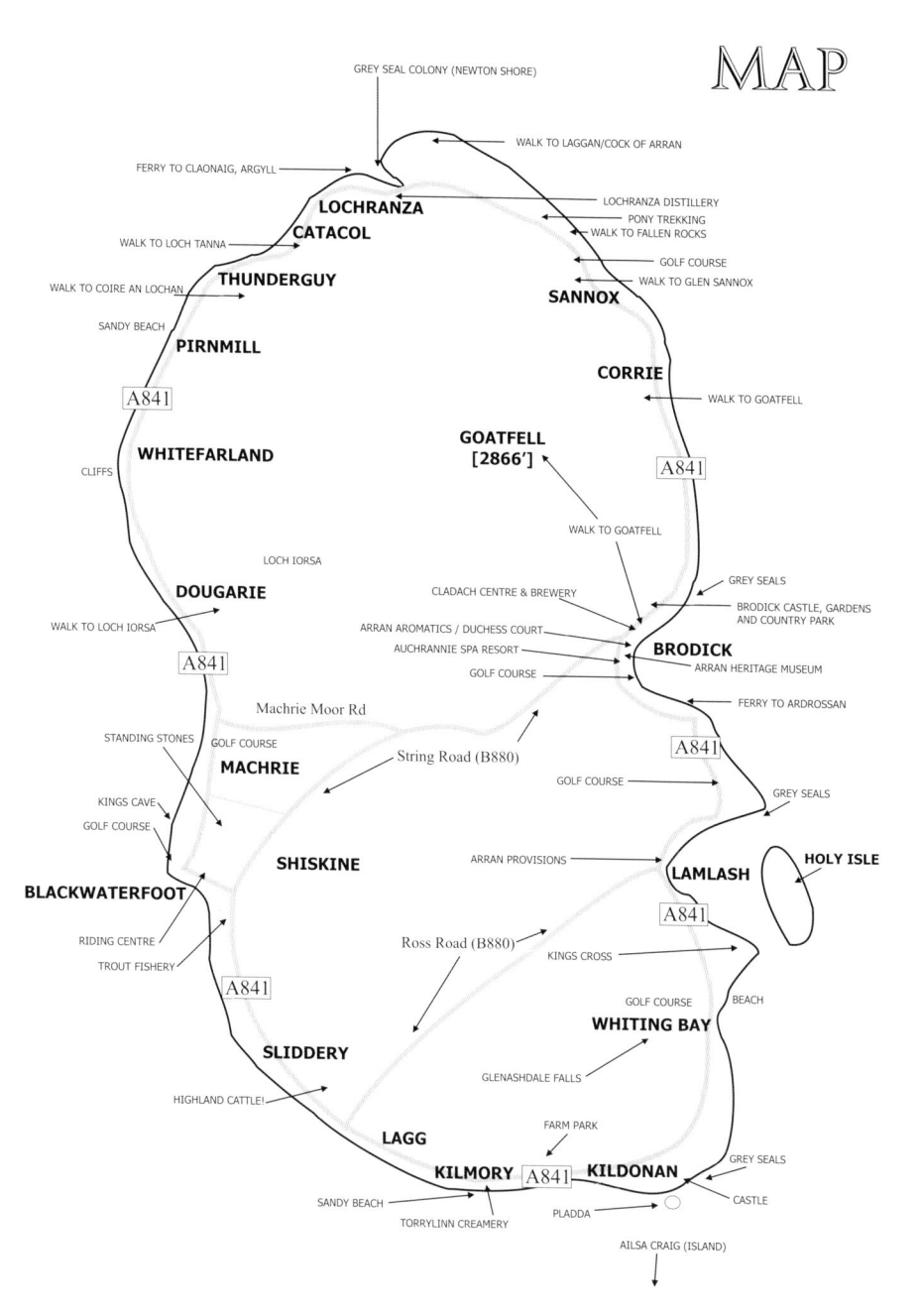

FAQs

Photographic.

"Where can I buy Camera Film & Batteries?"
Most village shops and some craft shops sell limited supplies of each. You can buy APS film at the Brodick Pharmacy as well as 8mm Camcorder Tape.

"Is there anywhere to get photos developed?"
The aforementioned Chemists, Brodick Pharmacy, offer one-hour film developing services.

"What about Digital Cameras?"
You can get your camera's "Smart-Media" card transferred to CD Rom at Arran Graphics, in the rear of "Inspirations of Arran", Brodick. The charge is £10 per visit and the office is open Mon-Fri 9 - 5. Allow 24 hours. For other card types, you may have problems finding replacements on Arran.

Emergencies

"I'm a member of the A.A / R.A.C - are they represented on the island?"
Angus Lambie Motor Engineers is the island's representative and operates a 23½ -hour service, as written on his recovery vehicles. It is not known what the remaining ½ hour is used for, and it's possibly best not to ask! If you need emergency recovery or breakdown services, call your usual helpline number first.

"Who do I call in an emergency?"
The usual 999 (or 112) services are available on the island, which include both the Coastguard and Arran Mountain Rescue. If you just want to talk to a local police officer, call 302574 or 302573 (this number will divert your call to Kilmarnock if the Arran Police station is unmanned.

Miscellaneous Queries

"Can I rent golf clubs on Arran?"
Generally, no. However, ask your accommodation provider - they may lend you a set or know how to borrow someone else's!

"Where can I buy a Sunday Newspaper?"
Newspapers on Sundays arrive much later on the island and are usually available in Brodick and Lamlash by around 11.00am, the other village shops a little later.

"Can I cash travellers cheques or change foreign currency anywhere?"
Aside from the main ferry and the banks which offer these services during normal hours, there is no bureau de change. However, larger hotels may exchange travellers cheques.

"I've bought, or intend to buy, more souvenirs/produce that I can carry off the island."
Call Arran Deliveries on 01475 676255 to arrange shipment to any UK address by courier. They take credit cards, too.

"In the winter season I got handed a boarding card as well as a ticket for the ferry, but in summer I just had a ticket. Why?
Can I get back to you on that one?

PEAKS

Beinn Nuis → Beinn Tarsuinn → Beinn a'Chliabhain → Beinn Capulford (?) → A'Chir → Cir Mhor → Goat Fell

ARRAN'S MOUNTAINS - as seen from the Brodick◇Lamlash Road

Note that this view includes the top three highest peaks on Arran.

Name	Height in ft/m	Gaelic Translation
Goatfell	2866' / 874m	"Mountain of Wind" / Goat Peak
Bheinn Tarsuinn	2710' / 826m	Transverse Hill
Cir Mhor	2621' / 799m	Big Comb
A'Chir	2335' / 712m	The Comb
Beinn a'Chliabhain	2142' / 653m	Creel Mountain / Hill of the Basket
Beinn Capulford	*6'1" / 1.85m*	

ISLAND TRIVIA

Geography

"Scotland in miniature?" - The island of Arran would fit into Scotland 183 times.

The island of Arran takes up 0.00028% of the earth's land mass.

Arran has the same population density as the state of Florida

Arran would fit into the USA about 21,932 times and into the Grand Canyon 13 times. The island is 961 times smaller than the state of California.

Mount Everest is just over 10 times higher than Arran's highest peak, Goatfell (2866').

Roads

Arran's roads have no permanent traffic lights, roundabouts or double yellow lines.

It is slightly quicker to drive **anti-clockwise** around the island.

Arran has no full-time traffic wardens or car- park attendants.

LPG Gas for newly-converted cars is now available in Brodick

Visitors

Arran's has around 250,000 visitors a year.

Some self-catering units on Arran are the holiday homes of people who live as far away as the USA, Asia and Australia.

The Arran Folk Festival attracts acts, and visitors, from all over the world.

Obscurities

Arran's mail often arrives by a converted fishing trawler in the winter.

There is no natural "blue" rhododendron species, although almost every other colour is represented.

Wooleys Bakery makes enough oatcakes in one year to reach, end-to-end, from their shop in Brodick, to the Clyde Tunnel in Glasgow.

VISITOR CENTRE CHECKLIST

(NOT IN ANY SPECIFIC ORDER)

- [ ] **BRODICK CASTLE, GARDENS & COUNTRY PARK**
  BRODICK

- [ ] **ISLE OF ARRAN DISTILLERY & VISITOR CENTRE**
  LOCHRANZA

- [ ] **ARRAN AROMATICS & DUCHESS COURT SHOPS**
  BRODICK

- [ ] **THE CLADACH CENTRE & ISLE OF ARRAN BREWERY**
  BRODICK

- [ ] **THE AUCHRANNIE SPA RESORT**
  BRODICK

- [ ] **BALMICHAEL VISITOR CENTRE**
  SHISKINE

- [ ] **TORRYLINN CREAMERY**
  KILMORY

- [ ] **HOLY ISLE**
  LAMLASH BAY

- [ ] **ISLE OF ARRAN HERITAGE MUSEUM**
  BRODICK

- [ ] **ARRAN PROVISIONS (PATERSON ARRAN LTD)**
  LAMLASH

- [ ] **SOUTH BANK FARM PARK**
  Nr KILMORY

- [ ] **PORT-NA-LOCHAN FISHERY**
  BLACKWATERFOOT

FURTHER READING

'Historical' Books

Arran Shipwrecks	Donald Johnston
The Pictorial History of Arran	Andrew Boyle
The Isle of Arran	Ken Hall

'Walking' Books

Walking on the Isle of Arran	Paddy Dillon
18 Walks on the Isle of Arran	Sandra Bentley

General Books on the island

Arran - Behind The Scenes	Gillean Bussell
The Isle of Arran	Robert McLellan / Norman Newton
Arran & The Clyde Islands	Scottish Natural Heritage
Discovering Arran	Alastair Gemmell
The Milestones of Arran	Ruth & Alan Thompson

Maps & Guides

Ordnance Survey Landranger #69 Isle of Arran (1:50,000)
Ordnance Survey Leisure #37 Isle of Arran (1: 25,000)
The Official Tourist Map - Isle of Arran   Ayrshire & Arran Tourist Board

Arran Bird Report	Arran Natural History Society
The Arran Flora	Arran Natural History Society

Contact Sources:

The Arran Index Telephone Directory   (by The Arran Banner)
The '@rran Directory'   Arran Graphics & Computers Ltd
(contains website, email and fax numbers for businesses & individuals)

Multimedia

The Isle of Arran CD Rom   Ben Capulford

There is also a VHS video, entitled "The Isle of Arran" available throughout the island.

INDEX

Auchrannie Spa	45
B&B	23,50,54,59,62,69,81
Balmichael Visitor Centre	70
Banks	42,43
Banner, The Arran	26,40
Boats	41,53,66
Brewery, The Arran	47
Brodick Castle	41,47,49,50
Bus Services	18,19
Business Services	32,33
Camping	23,50,54,59,69,81
Car Hire	18,20
Cheese	46,80
Cladach Visitor Centre	47
Clearances	64
Climate	25
Co-Op	40,54
Cycling	19
Distillery	65,68
Driving	16,17
Eating Out	20,50,55,59,62,68,74,77,81
Email	33
Emergencies	52
FAQs	90-91
Ferry Services	14,15,39,66
Fishing	53, 71, 77
Glen Sannox	61
Glenashdale	58
Goatfell	48,60
Golf	44,52,58,61,65,73,76
Guest Houses	24,50,55,59,62,69,81
Halls	28
Hitch Hiking	20
Holy Isle	53,58
Hotels	24,50,55,59,62,69,74,81
Internet	33

INDEX (CONT...)

Kings Cave	74
Lochranza Castle	66
Mail	32,43
Maps	84-88
Mountain Ridges	92
Museum	46
Mustard	54
North Sannox	62
Petrol	19,39,42,56,72
Photocopying	34
Pony Trekking	62,72
Post Offices	32,43,53,57,66,72,79,80
Roads	16,17,71
Self Catering	24,50,59,62,9,74,78,81
Standing Stones	76
STB	21,22
Taxis	18,19
Telephones	32,34
Tourism	12,13,21,22
Trivia	93
Visitor Centre Check List	94
Weather	25
What's On	25
Whisky	65,68
Wildlife	29,30,31,
Youth Hostels	23,69

SPOTTERS NOTES

Use this section to note down any sightings of birds, plants and animals on your travels around the island.

What	Where	When	What	Where	When

WALKERS NOTES

Use this section to remind you of walks you've done, or mountains you've climbed.

Walk / Mountain	Time Taken	Comments

GENERAL NOTES

GENERAL NOTES